G000042658

Family Art

Family Life Series

Edited by Martin Richards, Ann Oakley, Christina Hardyment and Jackie Burgoyne.

Published

Forthcoming

Family Art

PHILIP PACEY

Polity Press

Copyright © Philip Pacey 1989

First published 1989 by Polity Press
in association with Basil Blackwell.

Editorial Office:
Polity Press, Dales Brewery, Gwydir Street
Cambridge CB1 2LJ, UK

Marketing and production:
Basil Blackwell Ltd
108 Cowley, Road, Oxford OX4 1JF, UK

Basil Blackwell Inc.
3 Cambridge Center
Cambridge, MA 02142, USA

All rights reserved. Except for the quotation of short passages for the
purposes of criticism and review, no part of this publication may be
reproduced, stored in a retrieval system, or transmitted, in any form
or by any means, electronic, mechanical, photocopying, recording or
otherwise, without the prior permission of the publisher.

Except in the United States of America, this book is sold subject to
the condition that it shall not, by way of trade or otherwise, be lent,
resold, hired out, or otherwise circulated without the publisher's
prior consent in any form of binding or cover other than that in
which it is published and without a similar condition including this
condition being imposed on the subsequent purchaser.

ISBN 0 7456 0664 4

British Library Cataloguing in Publication Data
A CIP catalogue record for this book is available from the British
Library.

Library of Congress Cataloging-in-Publication Data
Pacey, Philip.
  Family art.
  (Family life series)
  Bibliography: p.
  Includes index.
    1. Family—Miscellanea. 2. Family festivals.
3. Folk art. 4. Collectibles. I. Title. II. Series:
Family life series (Oxford, England)
GT2420.P33 1989   306.85   89-9815
ISBN 0-7456-0664-4

Typeset in 11 on 13pt Palacio
by Downdell Limited, Oxford.
Printed in Great Britain by
T.J. Press (Padstow) Ltd, Padstow, Cornwall.

'The home is a craft cultivated by all its members'.
Mihaly Csikszentmihalyi and Eugene Rochberg-Halton.
The meaning of things: domestic symbols and the self (1981)

Contents

Acknowledgements

This book would not have been written without the original inspiration of Eske Mathiesen, to whom I am also grateful for his continuing cooperation and encouragement. That it has achieved publication is due to Anthony Burton of the Bethnal Green Museum of Childhood for saying the right word in the right ear at the right time, and to Christina Hardyment (whose ear it was), who has been a stimulating and sympathetic editor.

I would also like to thank Birgit Kågström Janson of the Carl Larsson-gården, Sundborn, Sweden, for helpfully commenting on a draft of Chapter 5.

The many quotations in the text are fully acknowledged in the notes to each chapter. For permission to make use of certain longer passages, or of several passages, I am grateful to the following: Oxford University Press Inc., for permission to quote from *A pattern language: towns/buildings/construction* by Christopher Alexander. Copyright © 1977 by Christopher Alexander; St. Martin's Press Inc. and Curtis Brown Associates Ltd, for permission to quote from *Jewish family celebrations* by Arlene Rossen Cardozo. Copyright © 1982 by Arlene Rossen Cardozo; William Heinemann Ltd and Viking Penguin Inc., for permission to quote from *Home: a short history of an idea* by Witold Rybczynski. Copyright © 1986 by Witold Rybczynski; Harper & Row Publishers, Inc., for permission to quote from *The passing of the modern age* by John Lukacs; Faber & Faber Ltd, for permission to quote from Lucy Boston's *Green Knowe* series of children's books; Manchester University Press, for permission

Acknowledgements

to quote from *The classic slum* and *A ragged schooling* by Robert Roberts; and Camden Press for permission to quote from *Putting myself in the picture* by Joe Spence.

For permission to reproduce the illustrations I would like to thank the Trustees of The National Gallery, London (Plate 1); the Museum of English Naive Art, Bath (Plate 2); the Kunsthalle, Hamburg (Plate 3); the Rijkmuseum, Amsterdam (Plate 4); Albert Bonniers Förlag AB, Stockholm, Sweden (Plate 5); the Nationalmuseum, Stockholm and Statens Konstmuseer (Plate 6); Den Fynske Landsby, Odense (Plate 8); Greenfield Village and the Henry Ford Museum, Dearborn, Michigan (Plate 9); the Documentary Photography Archive, Manchester (Plates 10 and 11); Ken and Kate Baynes (Plate 14); and Hodder and Stoughton (Plate 15).

1

What is Family Art?

'Family art' is an unfamiliar term that is not in any dictionary; nor is it referred to in books on art or studies of the family. But family art is neither new nor rare. It happens without having to be labelled; people make it almost without noticing; because it goes unnoticed, unsung, unstudied, it has not needed to be named. By and large, this is as it should be, and I would suggest that 'family art' is a term that should be used sparingly. But at the same time a book about it is, I believe, more than justified, and not simply by my desire to share the shock of recognition I experienced when I first saw the words 'family art' emerge in the course of the translating of an essay from Danish into English.[1] It is justified by what family art can tell us about family and home; because family art takes us beyond materialism and shows us how to recreate our world and cultivate the significance of objects and artefacts; and not least because stepping back to look at family art offers an opportunity to remind ourselves that creativity is as natural to human beings as breathing itself. Family art insists that there is a role for art in everyday life; it tells us a good deal about what art is, and it confirms that everyone is 'a special kind of artist'.

But what is family art? Eske Mathiesen, the Danish author of the text just referred to, has written that 'every family creates its own visual traditions' that 'embody the family's understanding and love of one another'. As examples of what can contribute to a family's visual tradition, he cites 'the setting out of birthday tea tables'; flower arrangements; Christmas decorations;

1

greetings cards; and not least, the family album in which 'every photograph is a peephole into the life of the past'. 'Every home', he says,

> is a living museum. It is filled with pictures and things, which in one way or another have a place in the life of the family and tell us something about it.[2]

But if words like 'tradition' and 'museum' suggest that family art is solely concerned with recalling the past, this is not so; rather, family art contributes to a continual creating of a world in the here and now, a responsive world of love, which, creating itself in the present, embodies its own history. Love does not willingly forget; without 'living in the past', it treasures its past which enriches its present; it carries its past into the future. Family art mourns and recalls the dead, facilitating the expression of grief. But for the living, and not least for any children in the family, family art is the creating of the home as that portion of the world which is one's own habitat, known and loved and familiar, bearing one's own marks of ownership or use, harbouring one's own things, including things made or chosen especially for you, tokens of affection and of belonging.

Family art could be defined as the visual aspect of family *culture*, which the Smithsonian Institution's Family Folklore Program has divided into four categories: *verbal*; *written* (such as letters, diaries, etc.); *behavioural* (principally ceremonies and rituals); and *visual*.[3] Family art encompasses not only the last of these in its entirety, but also the visual dimension of ceremonies and rituals (that are sometimes recorded in family photographs). Indeed, the nature of family art is such that it resists narrow, excluding, definition; it contributes to the essential indivisibility of home and family; it has the potential to contribute to the construction, maintenance, and integrity of larger percepts — community and civilization, reality and world. Walt Whitman understood how the different elements of a family's culture, together comprising a home and a way of life, contribute to the growing child's unfolding sense of the world as actual and reliable, and to the confidence which he or she acquires for life:

The family usages, the language, the company, the furniture,
　　the yearning and swelling heart,
Affection that will not be gainsay'd, the sense of what is
　　real . . .[4]

This same sense of home as most especially real is quaintly but beautifully expressed in the following verse, entitled 'Home Poem', apparently written by an 11-year-old girl in Iowa in 1936:

Home ain't a place that gold can buy or get up in a minute
Afore its home there's got t'be aheap a'livin' in it;
Within the walls there's got t'be some babies born, and then
Right there ye've got to 'bring 'em upt' women good, an' men.
And gradjerly as time goes on ye find ye wouldn't part
With anything they ever used they've grown into yer heart
The old chairs, the playthings, too, the little shoes they wore
Ye hoard; an if ye could ye'd keep the thumbmarks on the
　　door.[5]

Family art is a family's endless giving to itself a home — a home in which the family can recognize itself, and which for each member of the family reaffirms that this is where they belong, because here they are loved for what they are. Such a home is a world; would that the world could be such a home.

And yet, sadly, *not* every home is a 'living museum'. Take this English drawing room of 1855 for example, as described by Mrs Gaskell in *North and South*:

> There was no one in the drawing-room. It seemed as though no one had ever been in it since the day when the furniture was bagged up with as much care as if the house was to be overwhelmed with lava, and discovered a thousand years hence. The walls were pink and gold; the pattern on the carpet represented bunches of flowers on a lit ground, but it was carefully covered up in the centre by a linen drugget, glazed and colourless. The window-curtains were lace; each chair and sofa had its own particular veil of netting or knitting. Great alabaster groups occupied every flat surface, safe from dust under their glass shades. In the middle of the room, right under the bagged-up

3

chandelier, was a large circular table, with smartly bound books arranged at regular intervals round the circumference of its polished surface, like gaily coloured spokes of a wheel. Everything reflected light, nothing absorbed it. The whole room had a painfully spotted, spangled, speckled look about it, which impressed Margaret so unpleasantly that she was hardly conscious of the peculiar cleanliness required to keep everything so white and pure in such an atmosphere, or of the trouble that must be willingly expended to secure the effect of icy, snowy discomfort. Wherever she looked there was evidence of care and labour, but not care and labour to procure ease, to help on habits of tranquil home enjoyment; solely to ornament and then to preserve ornament from dirt or destruction.[6]

Times have changed, yet many modern homes express little of the uniqueness of their inhabitants; they are show-rooms for the contents of large stores or mail-order catalogues, or they mimic the taste of womens' and home magazines, or of 'good' design. Perhaps only a display of family photos on the television can be regarded as belonging uniquely to the family; even this may be swept away. Yet, as Witold Rybczynski has noted in his book *Home: a short history of an idea*:

Hominess is not neatness. Otherwise everyone would live in replicas of the kinds of sterile and impersonal homes that appear in interior-design and architectural magazines. What these spotless rooms lack, or what crafty photographers have carefully removed, is any evidence of human occupation. In spite of the artfully placed vases and casually arranged art books, the imprint of their inhabitants is missing. These pristine interiors fascinate and repel me. Can people really live without clutter? How do they stop the Sunday papers from spreading over the living room? How do they manage without toothpaste tubes and half-used soap bars in their bathrooms? Where do they hide the detritus of their everyday lives?[7]

As Rybczynski implicitly suggests, such interiors, with their law of tidiness and exclusion of the personal, seem certain to inhibit, if not to prohibit, spontaneous family life; whatever they have been shaped by, it is not that.

Rybczynski's book could be described as a history of *comfort*.

A striking feature of Mrs Gaskell's description of the drawing room, quoted above, is the characterization of the room's overall effect as of a calculated 'icy, snowy discomfort', and the contrasting of this with 'ease' and 'tranquil home enjoyment'. Rybczynski recognizes that comfort involves more than the ease of the body; to feel fully at home we need to feel *comforted*, reassured; a function of personal possessions in the home is to extend the process of transforming a house (or dwelling) *into* home *beyond* the provision of merely physical comfort. After asking himself the puzzled, distressing question 'Can people really live without clutter?' Rybczynski seeks comfort in contemplation of the objects which surround him where he sits writing:

> Many personal mementos, photographs and objects – reliquaries of family, friends, and career – fill my study. A small gouache of a young man – myself – seated in a Formentera doorway. A sepia-coloured photograph of a German zeppelin hovering over Boston on the way to Lakehurst. A photograph of my own house under construction. A Gujarati wall hanging. A framed note from a Famous Man. A corkboard, messages, telephone numbers, visiting cards, yellowing unanswered letters and forgotten bills. A black sweater, some books, and a leather briefcase are lying on the daybed which stands on the other side of the room. My writing desk is an old one. Although it is not a particularly valuable antique, its elegance recalls a time when letter writing was a leisurely art, carefully performed with pen and ink blotter. I feel a little ashamed as I scrawl untidy notes on legal pads of cheap yellow paper. On the desk, in addition to the mess of books and paper, are a heavy brass padlock used as a paperweight, a tin can full of pencils, a cast-iron Sioux Indian-head bookend, and a silver snuffbox with the likeness of George II on its cover. Did it once belong to my grandfather? I cannot remember. The plastic cigarette box next to it must have – in addition to the prewar Polish marque, it carries his initials.[8]

Here is a different sort of comfort – an environment which responds to personal identity and family associations as a comfortable chair responds to the requirements of the body.

5

Family art creates home from inside, through inhabiting, so that home reflects and strengthens personal and family identities. Its personal and relatively private meanings are overlaid on public 'languages' in which, for instance, houses of different kinds speak of degrees of wealth or social status, and the furniture, possessions, customs and 'lifestyles' similarly tell of success and security. The spirit of family art has nothing to do with the extravagance and swank of 'conspicuous consumption', but on the other hand it is not at odds with the need for families to comfort and reassure themselves that all is well, that their survival is as assured as it can be, that they are accepted within their community. Thus family art need not necessarily be opposed to public idioms of taste, decor, or style; rather, it *adds* to the home another dimension of visual significance and of comfort. Family art releases creativity to enhance and enrich the home and to make of it a more complete and eloquent statement, liberating us to inhabit our surroundings rather than merely camping in them. In an age of commercialism, in which it is possible to buy in not only complete interiors, but also, for instance, presents and greetings cards for every occasion, and even an entire funeral, family art can be seen as a rearguard action against complete capitulation, an insistence that commerce be kept in its place. Similarly, where pressures to conform seek to encroach too far, family art represents a bastion of liberty, a strong but gentle *agent provocateur* which does not seek to overthrow but merely to limit the reach of those powers it itself is threatened by.

Family art is the visible aspect of family culture; a family's culture is not unrelated to the culture of society at large, or to those ethnic, religious or other distinct strands of society to which the family belongs. Most families incorporate elements of the traditions inherited by both wife and husband, brought together into a synthesis enriched by variation and innovation; not infrequently, features of the family life of their childhood, that, as adolescents striving towards their own individuality, they had resented, or as independent adults had had no need of, are revived by parents in response to and for the sake of their own children.[9] Families are organic cells of civilization as a

6

whole, and contribute to its continuity and regeneration. The vital element of *creativity* — in the making of free choices and new syntheses as well as in the originating of what is, or seems, entirely without precedent — and in its ability to rise above rules and conventions at least by reinterpreting and breathing new life into custom and tradition — will be a principal theme of this book. Family culture (which must include personal privacy and expression) nourishes and accommodates members of the family as individual creative spirits but in a social context in which creativity is seen to consist of more than mere self expression and is thus distinguished from selfishness.

This book is *not* an attempt to write a definitive *history* of family art. Any such attempt would be foolhardy indeed, given that professional historians disagree among themselves regarding the history of the family. It has been suggested that the close-knit and affectionate 'nuclear' family is a relatively recent and essentially 'Modern' phenomenon,[10] and that childhood — a central feature and almost the *raison d'être* of such families — scarcely existed as a concept before the seventeenth century and only gradually developed thereafter.[11] These ideas of course dovetail neatly enough with the broader interpretation of the 'Modern' period as characterized by individuality, inwardness, and self-awareness, and thus by the cultivation of privacy, in contrast to the living of life almost entirely in public.[12] The depicting of a panorama of the past with such bold brush strokes can perhaps be regarded as an equivalent of the scientist's hypothesis, at least in that it has to be subjected to close scrutiny, rigorously tested, weighed against the evidence, and almost certainly modified to a greater or lesser extent (if not wholly abandoned). So far as the history of the family and of childhood are concerned, this process is well under way.[13]

The evidence of family art does not in itself conflict with these theories. Of course, I have been limited to such evidence as has been, in one way or another, within my reach; within that sphere I have been limited to such evidence as *survives*. But almost by definition, family art does not survive. It is preserved in the family or not at all. Often it is truly ephemeral: that is, it is created by or within a family for a particular occasion; it is enmeshed with, or indeed *is*, that occasion, and is similarly vulnerable to the passing of time. Or, part of the living process and the clutter of family life, it is one of the first things to be tidied away before a room is portrayed or photographed. Even relatively costly, accomplished, and (one would have thought) permanent portraits have proved to be surprisingly vulnerable. Thus for example it has been estimated that during the 1840s at least 3,500 portraits were painted in Berlin alone; 100 years later only 500 of these could be traced. In explaining this, Kate Gläser referred to a Berlin proverb, according to which a certain number of family removals from one house to another have the same effect on the family's possessions as a fire; many families had been dispersed, and portraits dear to the generation that remembered the individuals depicted meant little to later descendants.[14]

In its contribution to an overview of the history of the family, therefore, family art cannot reasonably be expected to do a great deal more than confirm the fact that the kind of families that produce it, and the kind of home it is produced in, have existed for at least a century and a half. Evidence from this period, and soundings into earlier times, *do* suggest that family art can be associated with a tradition of domesticity which was vividly prefigured by Dutch middle-class homes of the seventeenth century, and in which individuality has been nurtured within the family, *and* that it is a reflection of family identity and (in many cases) self-confidence, *but also* that it has been facilitated by the wider choice of commodities and by new modes of expression (notably photography) which have become available during the nineteenth and twentieth centuries. To a large extent, then, this study of family art is about how families interact with material culture in a materialist consumer society, and about how families that have the will to do so use material things and means of expression in their own way, in spite of pressures to conform.

This is the tradition, 'Western' and predominantly middle class, which I have been born into, am familiar with, and cannot avoid writing from within. It is this tradition that has presented me with my evidence. However, it is not my wish to be drawn into identifying family art too exclusively with this tradition or with any strand or historical period within it. On the contrary, the underlying purpose of this book is to reveal in family art values and strategies, and in particular a role for creativity, which need not be identified with any particular time or place or cultural tradition. Indeed, evidence of family art in other historical periods, and of varieties of family art in other cultures, would simply add weight to the argument.

And the argument is this: that family art demonstrates that creativity can and should be an integral part of everybody's everyday life; that as such, it can and does serve the family, not simply by enriching its private culture but also by facilitating interaction between family and community, home and infinity, life spans, history, and eternity; and that, furthermore, it has the potential to serve 'families' however defined, including families that recreate themselves (by regrouping, embracing friends, or disengaging from the charades, beloved of playwrights, of merely dutiful, explosive reunions), groups, communities, and ultimately, the world as family. Only by living creatively can humankind, *all of us*, make the world home.

2

Images of Family and Home:
Peeping into the Past

Looking back into the past, experiencing it through its picturing
of itself, we can sometimes experience a *frisson* of recognition
and find ourselves foreseeing a future which is our present.
Paintings, both of families and of domestic interiors, as well as
interiors themselves where these survive, offer vivid glimpses
of scenes that for many of us, in Europe and North America in
particular, reveal antecedents of our own ways of life. To peep
in this way is not of course to enter fully into the lives of our
ancestors; what we can see is only a glimpse of a larger world.
Examination of the evidence can increase our understanding
and correct misunderstandings, but the world of the past is
firmly and tantalizingly past – we cannot bring it back to life;
straining our ears to eavesdrop we cannot quite hear what is
being said; prying through cracks in doors that artists have
obligingly left open, we will never be able to see what is out of
our sight or hidden from view.

Family scenes and domesticity first enter European art through
the back door left open by the religiosity of the Middle Ages.
The Nativity and the Flight into Egypt occasioned the production
of countless images of a 'nuclear' family, set in some of the
earliest domestic interiors to be depicted in art. The birth and
childhood of the Virgin and of St. John provided pretexts for
additional scenes of domesticity. Contemporary families appeared discreetly in fifteenth century altar-pieces and stained-
glass windows in which the donor and his family are depicted

10

beneath or in a corner of a religious subject. In sixteenth-century English church monuments, the whole family (living as well as dead) sometimes cluster round the figures of the parents, but these funeral effigies, public rather than private statements, prolong those aspects of medieval civilization which determined that 'all things in life were of a proud or cruel publicity'.[1] Portraits, which only the aristocracy could afford, presented images of rank and property, of ancestral continuity; almost heraldic in function, they sometimes incorporated the family arms; even when displayed within the walls of palaces and great houses, they existed not so much to refresh the family's private memory but to blazon forth the family's lineage.

However, beginning perhaps with Van Eyck's 'The Marriage of the Arnolfini' of 1434 – the family portrait as marriage certificate (a public statement) and wedding picture (a private record) – and with his portrait of his wife Margaretha (inscribed on the frame 'co[n]ius m[eu]s Joha[nn]es me c[om]plevit an[n]o 1439, 17 Junii': 'my husband painted me on June 17th 1439') – it is possible to trace a line of development that was to lead to family art. Other portraits of conjugal couples – such as Lorenzo Lotto's 'Family Portrait' of around 1523 in the Hermitage – and of families, appear to offer evidence of loving attachment and of domesticity, and in particular of an appreciation of wife and mother as more than a means of continuing paternal lineage. However, it has been suggested that such pictures, influenced by religious iconography and its portrayal of the Virgin, anticipated and ultimately helped to bring about change rather than reflecting established practice.[2] Perhaps with its help, then, depictions of families and of children separated themselves from religious art, and gradually family groups unfroze into informal scenes, known as 'conversation pieces', which portrayed families at ease, caught in the middle of everyday life, and in their own homes. A 'flood of pictures of families' in the sixteenth and seventeenth centuries marked the 'secularization of the portrait':

> the family contemplates itself in the home . . . The need is felt to
> fix the present condition of that family, sometimes also recalling

Plate 1 *The Marriage of the Arnolfini*. 1434. Jan Van Eyck (Courtesy of the Trustees of The National Gallery, London)

the memory of the dead by means of a picture or an inscription on the wall.[3]

Whereas the great families had their portraits painted by well-known artists, lesser families followed their example as best they could, and even well down the social ladder the families of clergy and local dignitaries could benefit from the services of, often, itinerant portrait painters, of varying degrees of accomplishment. The visit of such a portraitist, who 'took likenesses for fifteen shillings a head', is described in Goldsmith's *The Vicar of Wakefield*.[4] He is employed by the Primrose family precisely because he has already portrayed a neighbouring family:

> As this family and ours had long a sort of rivalry in point of taste, our spirit took the alarm at this stolen march upon us, and notwithstanding all I could say, and I said much, it was resolved that we should have our pictures done too.

Much thought was then given by the Primroses as to how best 'to shew the superiority of our taste', and they resolved 'to have something in a brighter style' and to be painted together

> in one large historical family piece. This would be cheaper, since one frame would serve for all, and it would be infinitely more genteel; for all families of any taste were now drawn in the same manner.

A further social point is made by the inclusion, at his request, of the Squire ('an honour too great to escape envy'), but alas! the Primroses' pretensions are deflated when it turns out that the completed painting is too large to hang in the house and has to be left leaning 'in a most mortifying manner' against the kitchen wall, 'the jest of our neighbours'.

Even allowing for Goldsmith's clear desire to poke fun at the Primroses, there can be no doubt that the commissioning of portraits could have a good deal to do with status, but this need not have been invariably so. Surely we should not doubt that portraits were treasured by families as 'likenesses' reflecting their mutual affection and togetherness. In contrast with the Primroses' too-large painting, clearly intended to serve a

Plate 2 *Family Group* c.1880. An oil painting from Liverpool, clearly the work of a relatively unsophisticated portrait painter, and possibly depicting a rising merchant and his family. (Museum of English Naive Art, Bath)

primarily public function (and for the enhancement of which they were only too happy to temporarily extend the family), portrait miniatures and silhouettes were popular in the eighteenth century and until the coming of photography. In their provision of both relatively inexpensive and of small-scale, easily portable portraits, they anticipated photography. Although sometimes displayed, usually in groups, miniatures were often contained in hinged, folding frames, so they could be easily and safely carried and then stood up like an open book, or they were incorporated in jewellery or personal accessories. Art historians have weighed up the respective achievements of those miniature painters who were patronized by royalty and the aristocracy, but have showed little interest in who else used miniatures, how, and at what cost. But that miniatures were not restricted to the rich is shown by a painting by Peter Fendi of Vienna, a Biedermaier portraitist who himself painted miniatures as well as larger paintings. His 'Die arme Offizierswitwe' ('The poor officer's widow') of 1836 depicts the widow, who is shown with her small children in her single garret room, with a framed miniature of her dead husband open in front of her.[5] In America, silhouette portraits could be obtained from an itinerant 'Taker of profile Likenesses' for 25 cents for two profiles of one person, unframed, or 50 cents to 2 dollars framed, in 1806.[6]

Silhouettes, though fashionable, were simultaneously regarded as essentially cheap substitutes for portraits in oils, as is indicated by the fact of their being named after Etienne Silhouette, the French Minister of Finance under Louis XIV who was notorious for preaching economy at a time when extravagance was rampant, and indeed his name was associated with anything cheap and tawdry. Like miniatures, silhouettes were most frequently employed to produce likenesses of individuals, although silhouette 'conversation pieces' of whole families were not unknown. An engraving in J. C. Lavater's popular *Essays on physiognomy* which was published in an English edition in 1794 shows a family making its own silhouettes; father is making a silhouette of mother, and the children are making a silhouette of the cat! Thus silhouettes may be seen to

15

have specifically foreshadowed photography in equipping families with a technique for producing their own likenesses which was inexpensive and could be attempted regardless of skill. It resembled photography too in its use of light, and its downfall may have been brought about not simply by photography but also by the advent of gas and electric lighting in place of candles and lamps, the intense side-lighting from which facilitated and no doubt stimulated the making of silhouettes.

The uses of, and demand for, portrait painting, and ways in which it anticipates photography, are most interestingly illuminated by the work of Mary Ellen Best, a nineteenth-century self-taught artist from a respectable English family.[7] Ellen Best's parents had had their portraits painted at the time of their marriage; Ellen later made copies of these portraits, as gifts for relatives, just as today we may have several photographic prints made from one negative for much the same purpose. Ellen gave her husband a self-portrait of herself at the time of *their* wedding; later she painted a portrait of him holding her self-portrait; later still she painted a watercolour of the family dining room in which the portrait containing the self-portrait can clearly be seen hanging on the wall: thus with these pictures Ellen created a series of mirrors, so to speak, catching and reflecting images of the family. Ellen used watercolour painting as a personal and family diary, by means of which she recorded her travels, the birth of children, and family life, and in due time she bequeathed to her children several albums of these watercolours, family albums, no less. Ellen also painted portraits on a semi-professional basis; perhaps by choice, but no doubt also because of the limited opportunities open to her as a woman, she worked only in watercolour, producing small, relatively inexpensive pictures that suited the pocket of the people she could most readily and happily work for, more often women than men, and sometimes servants.

Ellen Best's domestic watercolours constitute just one of several instances of members of well-to-do families taking up pencil or brush to produce informal sketches or more finished paintings of family life.[8] In both her art and her life — during which she and her husband travelled and resided in Europe —

she represents a link between England and the Europe of the Biedermeier period. The Biedermeier spirit was characterized by a cult of domesticity on the part of a bourgeoisie who flourished in the peace that followed the defeat of Napoleon. Biedermeier families liked to surround themselves with family portraits, pictures of their beloved homes (inside and out), and of favourite landscapes, and 'family members often attempted . . . modest depictions of their own in their eagerness to record their personal environment'.[9] A remarkable work by a Hamburg artist, Julius Oldach, a close contemporary of Ellen Best (although she was to outlive him by some 60 years), can be regarded as an early classic of family art, produced within and for the family and to mark a family occasion. His 'Family Tree' of 1828 in the Kunsthalle, Hamburg, was painted on the occasion of his parents' silver wedding, and features eleven portraits in medallions, linked by the trunk and branches of the family tree. Above and below are various scenes of family life. At the top, under the date 17 February 1803, is shown his parents' wedding, with, on either side, a birth and a baptism. In other scenes we see the artist himself working in his studio, mother giving out packed lunches to children setting out for school, a visit to a sick woman, piano practice, children's games, business being transacted, father sitting at a writing desk while the table is being laid in the background, meetings and greetings, the delivery of provisions, and at the centre, at the bottom (corresponding to the wedding scene at the top), the silver wedding anniversary feast. And thus, in the words of one observer:

> as if in a magic circle, the life of a day is completed and corresponds with the cycle of twenty-five years, like the coordination of the hour hand and the tiny minute hand in a well-oiled watch. The domestic scenes pass before our eyes like the automatic figures of a clock-tower, those ingenious masterpieces of clockwork which in Nuremberg or Strasbourg or elsewhere enchant the crowds at noon. In his modest picture, Oldach has caught the law which unites the microcosm of man's life with the macrocosm of nature. He has unfolded before our eyes the humble daily round, governed by the sound of a carillon, muffled by the clock's glass bell, much as Schiller, in his famous

Plate 3   *Family Tree*. 1828. Julius Oldach. (Kunsthalle, Hamburg)

Lied von der Glocke (1799) evoked, like the movements of a symphony, episodes of individual and social life which took place to the sound of a bell.[10]

Images of the family are only one element in family art, albeit an important one: they are one of the several and diverse ways in which family art expresses and reflects a family's identity. We will see that family art also contributes both to the daily round and to special festivities and occasions, as celebrated in Oldach's picture. Family images take their place in the home, whether they hang on the wall, stand on the mantelpiece, or are mounted in albums; besides them, the home contains other signs and objects which are charged with meaning and memories, and is itself, inside and out and altogether, a product of the family's inhabiting of it.

The family home is the locus of family art; it is the canvas on which family art paints itself, the theatre in which it is performed, the museum in which it is displayed. If most families inhabit a dwelling, over the design of which they could have no, or little control, that building then becomes raw material, to be converted by them into *home*. And if 'comfort' is one of our prime requirements of home, comfort involves more than physiological ease – as in the verb 'to comfort', it encompasses peace of mind, reassurance, well-being, the confirmation of identity and of belonging which are conferred by family art.

The word 'comfort' seems not to have been used to signify 'a level of domestic amenity' until the eighteenth century.[11] Indeed, the kind of continuum of comfort we have become accustomed to simply did not exist in medieval Europe; even for the wealthy, real comfort was a relatively rare pleasure, to be savoured in between trekking from one house to another, contrived with the aid of portable furniture and with little privacy. Changes came gradually, not so much as a result of technological development (medieval technology should not be underestimated) but of evolving ways of life. The idea of the house as purely residential and as the seat of family life arose from the locating of work (other than housework) elsewhere; it was enhanced by the practice of keeping children at home

19

longer, facilitated from the sixteenth century by the extension of formal schooling as an alternative to apprenticeship.

It is surely the capacity of interiors to reassure and to offer comfort that accounts for their potency as a subject of art. Like images of the family, domestic interiors make their appearance in art by way of, and as a background to, religious scenes, particularly from the later fifteenth century. From that century on, they become increasingly common.

> The gospel-writer, hitherto placed in a timeless setting, becomes a scribe at his desk, with a quill and an erasing-knife in his hand. At first he is placed in front of an ordinary ornamental curtain, but finally he is shown in a room where there are shelves lined with books: we have come from the gospel-writer to the author in his room . . .[12]

Scenes of the Nativity, and of the birth of the Virgin usher in the theme of childbirth; in Dutch and Flemish painting in particular, the architectural features and the furnishing of the interiors in which religious scenes are enacted, are more domestic than palatial; their detail is dwelt on with such obvious relish that its indisputable reality authenticates yet almost distracts from the explicitly religious subject matter of the paintings.

Holland in the seventeenth century merits special attention. The Dutch town house of that period, built by burghers, not princes, was perhaps a century ahead of its time in evolving the family home which was neither mansion nor hovel. And it was the house-proud Dutch who perfected the art of making pictures of domestic interiors, as seen in the masterpieces of Jan Vermeer and Pieter de Hooch in particular. The Dutch burghers, builders and artists together – and the housewives and servants whose role in the house is depicted in many paintings – succeeded in creating an archetype which still casts its serene spell around us.

Although 'hardly bristling with innovation',[13] at least in any technological sense, the Dutch town house, terraced and compact, advanced the subdivision of the house into rooms with particular functions, and into formal and informal areas, so that

Plate 4 *Interior with Two Women at a Linen Chest.* 1663. Pieter de Hooch. (Rijkmuseum, Amsterdam)

whereas the ground floor was thought of almost as an extension into the house of the street, the upper floors became relatively private. The outside walls at front and back, which bore no load, were pierced with windows, relieving the foundations of some of their own weight but also letting in light that artists were to rejoice in. The house was built for the family and, to an unprecedented degree, only for the family: the burghers worked elsewhere, and the hiring of servants was discouraged. The average number of people per house was no more than four or five: a married couple, children, maybe a single servant. Parents, especially the mother, could not but be involved in their children's upbringing, and most children lived at home

21

until they married. Love of family and love of home grew together: contemporary visitors noted how the Dutch prized three things above all else: first their children, second their homes, and third, their gardens. The garden behind the house became another, outdoor, family room. With few if any servants to assist, Dutch married women had 'the whole care and absolute management of all their Domestique',[14] and in the Dutch home, as depicted in paintings, the 'feminization of the home'[15] was made visible. *Housewives*, involved with their children as never before, were also responsible for cooking (with the result that the kitchen became an important room), and brought to the home both comfort and cleanliness. They, more than anyone, created domesticity, and it is domesticity, rather than merely domestic interiors, which de Hooch and Vermeer and other Dutch artists painted so evocatively.

In the Dutch house we see a home in which it is possible to imagine family art flourishing; indeed, many Dutch paintings of family and home almost seem to be family art although they were not produced within the family. Corporate national pride is certainly embodied in Dutch art of the time; what is missing from the paintings of domestic interiors are the tell-tale signs of a house being inhabited by one family rather than another; notably missing are the particular pictures within the pictures which would confirm for us that Dutch families commissioned paintings of themselves and their homes, to hang in their homes. The family has staked out its territory, laid claims to its privacy, but has not yet begun to use these in ways personal to it beyond making some choices of its own regarding its use of the common language of furnishing and decoration.

Family art is not a prerogative of a middle class; neither, for that matter, is art. 'Folk art' embraces the applied arts and crafts of people in, especially, pre-industrial rural communities: people who had little or no direct access to the fashionable arts. Folk art reveals the variety of skills which could be gathered, to a large extent from within the community, to make — among other things — home. It includes the building and decoration of houses and other buildings (such as barns), and the making and decorating of furniture, wagons, utensils, textiles, and indeed of everything essential to everyday life.

It is all too easy to romanticize the so-called 'organic' community; to imagine, for instance, that everyone was skilled in all sorts of crafts, and that people joyfully exercised a spontaneous creativity, albeit of an unsophisticated kind. Certainly people were, in a sense, indeed literally, closer to the production process; many of the things they owned would be made locally, by someone they knew. But there were specialists: the potter, the mason, the wheelwright, the blacksmith, the joiner; not everything for the home was made in the home or within the family circle; regional specialization, such as pottery manufacturing in Staffordshire, and the development of trade, increased the possibility that artefacts in the home might be bought at a fair or from a pedlar, having been made elsewhere. In America, perhaps because such portraits were commissioned *and survive* in great numbers (whereas in Britain they have been allowed to all but disappear), definitions of folk art are allowed to include portraits by itinerant painters: but at least some of these painters would turn their hand to other jobs – or else would turn their hand to portraits while more usually undertaking other work – thus blurring distinctions between roles and between categories of folk and 'fine', applied and figurative art. In 1844, while travelling near St Louis, Charles Dickens noted that many of the houses at Belleville

> had singularly bright doors of red and yellow; for the place had been lately visited by a travelling painter 'who got along' as I was told 'by eating his way'.[16]

That night Dickens stayed in an inn, where he noticed

> two oil portraits of the kit-cat size, representing the landlord and his infant son; both looking as bold as lions, and staring out of the canvas with an intensity that would have been cheap at any price. They were painted, I think, by the artist who had touched up the Belleville doors with red and gold paint; for I seemed to recognise his style immediately.[17]

But portraits in folk art are very much an exception that proves the rule. Folk art, as the name implies, is essentially a public art, the art of the folk rather than the family, even in its application to the dwelling and within the home. As a general rule, folk art is content to repeat itself rather than seeking to be different or original; in this way it continually reasserts communal tradition. Different communities have their own traditions: a method of construction, a mode of decoration, passed down from generation to generation with little variation. Not infrequently, personal initials are carved on a door lintel, a chest, a bed, but discreetly; artefacts *were* made for particular occasions, including family occasions – the daughter's wedding chest, for instance, containing bedlinen, maybe quilts, which she has made by herself or with her mother. And yet one senses that what is possible – even as regards portraits – is permitted by, and is made in obedience to and within the disciplines of, the communal tradition. In some communities, birth and baptismal certificates were allowed to be very elaborate, but were made not within the family but most usually by the local teacher who possessed the necessary skill in calligraphy. Weddings and other ceremonies were public rather than private occasions – occasions for the whole village, the rules for which were never departed from. The significance of the community is evident in the *veilées* or working evenings, common through much of Europe;[18] on winter evenings, partly to economize on firewood, the women, or women and men, would gather in one house or barn, to spin, knit or sew, and later perhaps to dance. Thus the making of even some of the more intimate household artefacts – clothes and bedlinen – took place in public. In America, *veilées* found their equivalent in the form of quilting 'bees'; whereas in quilt-making the design and preliminary work could be done at home, when it came to assembling the quilt help was needed, and women joined forces in occasions that, like the *veilées*, had a social as well as a utilitarian function.

Overwhelmingly the evidence of folk art suggests that the community is what mattered most: domestic interiors are expressions of the community and its range of crafts, rather than of the individual family. Two examples of what may reasonably be called folk art interiors, though surviving into the twentieth century, even to this day, illustrate folk art's application of public visual languages, shared by a community, to the domestic interior. The cabins of narrow boats on the English canals were the tiniest family homes imaginable, but were ingeniously planned and so snug and so richly decorated as to represent the epitome of cosiness. Yet their decoration followed a *schema* accepted by all boating families, and strictly limiting the family's contribution to a narrow range of choices. The painting of the cabin interior began with a buff yellow under-coat overall, combgrained with light oak scumble − if the boat was not owned by the family, this much would be done by the owner, but further embellishment was permitted at the boat-man's own expense. Further embellishment was indeed the norm, comprising repetition of motifs used also on the outside of the boat: patterns of roses, and, filling any suitable panels, landscapes featuring castles, which I have referred to elsewhere as 'the poor man's Claude Lorraines'.[19] (These scenes, like 'folk art' portraits, are derived from an altogether more fashionable and sophisticated idiom, but should not be dismissed as mere imitation: they represent a vigorous reinterpretation of their subject matter that the painters make truly their own, as distinct from a submissive acknowledgement or aping of superior taste. Indeed, such creativity is to be emphatically distinguished from the buying in of cheap versions or substitutes.) The boatmen could pay dock painters to do this, or might do it themselves. But when the painting was completed, dry, and varnished, the boatman's wife took over, and although in theory she had a completely free hand, she too followed established convention in hanging white crochet work from every shelf and ledge and by hanging from the walls, massed particularly behind the stove, her collection of souvenir plates with pierced 'lace' rims which echoed the crocheting and through which ribbons could be threaded. Very much part of the decor was a copper kettle and a capacious, highly decorated Measham teapot, greatly prized and handed down from mother to daughter. There was simply no desire to be different: if this mode of decoration was partially dictated by boat owners and the repertoire of dock painters, it was also voluntarily and happily embraced by the boat people who, a mobile community, were surely responsible for its evolution, and its perfection, for after all it represented the perfecting of the transformation of a mean living space into an Aladdin's cave. Although it could not be improved, its universal application meant that a family obliged by the owner to change boats, or a newly married couple taking charge of a boat for the first time, could feel instantly at home.[20]

A second example of a folk art interior can still be found on the Aran Islands. Here families, or to be precise, the Aran women, decorate rooms according to a communally accepted formula, the essence of which is the division of the walls into upper and lower halves of different colours separated by a strip of patterned wallpaper:

> One of the visual pleasures of these kitchens lies in the eccentric deployment of erratic quantities of paint. A dish cabinet or a door is painted from the same can of bright enameled paint as a small frame around a religious picture. The paint used to define a three-dimensional object may show up as a flat band around a deep-silled window. The movement of the colors − heavy and bright worked against luminous whitewash − compensates for the minimal skills in carpentry and masonry. The unpredictable color patches create a variety and liveliness in a house made up of white and two colors. But what colors! A kelly green and a chrome yellow, used in equal amounts. This kinetic, frugal paint scheme keeps the eye moving. When a paint can is opened, any object that looks woebegone receives a fresh coat. It's an anarchistic way to paint. Shelves made of cardboard receive the same irreverent, carefree enameling used on a door. The general effect is that paint equals freshening.[21]

While there clearly *is* scope for creativity here, it exists within the discipline of an overall scheme. Nor is it creativity for its own sake or for the sake of personal expression; the 'free' use of paint derives rather from necessity, from a wish to make the most of an open tin of paint and to leave nothing untouched. As in the narrow boat cabin, painting prepares the room for further embellishment; in this case, in addition to plates, mugs, and cups on a dresser, '80-cent purchases' such as plaster statuettes of the Virgin Mary, and framed religious pictures including portraits of 'at least one pope'. The placing of these in

26

the room, while 'witty and innately elegant', is also governed by convention. For example:

> There are three basic conventions for hanging pictures. The first is to hang the largest, always Jesus or Mary, about six inches from the ceiling, its top edge angled out from the wall. The second is to arrange groups in relation to the patterned divider which circles the room. The third convention relates objects to the doors and windows. A framed prayer, suspended by a string smack in the center above the door, does double duty, blessing the house and welcoming the visitor. None of the objects is placed only for decorative effect: these presences are like protectors spotted around . . . or connections. They create a stage set of cultural locators, defining the family's world as Catholic, Republic of Ireland, Gaelic-speaking, and their lineage as either Hernon, O'Brian or Concannon.[22]

And that is as close to the family's true identity as the room can take us: defined in relation to the community.

Yet there is something in this eye-witness account of an Aran home that can throw light, in advance, on a vital aspect of family art, an essential quality of home. And that is the appreciation of how the framed prayer above the door 'does double duty, blessing the house and welcoming the visitor'. The home which achieves privacy for its family, and within which and through which families articulate their unique identity and determine their own way of life, need not shut out the larger community altogether. The use of personal initials in folk art introduced a discreet, strictly limited token of individuality; individual and family portraits flourished in the context of American folk art in particular; family photographs could be introduced into the narrow boat cabin or the Aran home without upsetting or threatening the overall decor that linked the family to its community. Private and public could, and can, co-exist; they are after all interdependent.

What have these glimpses of the past revealed? In looking at family portraits, we have seen stiff and formal images of families, commissioned from professional artists of greater or lesser standing. We have also noticed relatively informal images, sometimes produced within the family itself, which in their informality anticipate the ways in which modern families use photography — though they scarcely begin to suggest how snapshots would break all the rules of portraiture. (Family photographs will be examined later in this book.) Paintings of domestic interiors and the evidence of folk art have allowed us to peep at families in their homes: homes which are family-scale, so to speak, which families clearly take a pride in and involve themselves in the arrangement and care of, but which nonetheless seem to lack a dimension of familial clutter and personal expression. It would be foolhardy to draw firm conclusions, though I find it hard to resist a sense of the family gathering its self-confidence; but we have begun to discern both what is, and what is not, quite, family art, and to appreciate that it has an ancestry older than we might otherwise have imagined.

3

'Homemaking'

Whether or not it is legitimate to think of the family gathering
its self-confidence between the seventeenth and eighteenth
centuries, there can be no question that at least since early in
the nineteenth century the family has been perceived as something to be reckoned with, an element in society too significant
to leave to its own devices. During this period the family has
been deluged with advice and instruction, in the form of
pamphlets, books and magazines; to what extent this flood of
publications may represent either an eruption of interest in the
family or a continuity of such interest that multiplied in
published (visible and lasting) form as a result of developments
in printing, publishing, and literacy, can be left to historians to
consider. Certainly household and marriage manuals were not
unknown in seventeenth century Holland, for instance. Advice
was forthcoming on planning a home, its architecture, and its
interior and decor; as was the case with the similarly plentiful
advice on motherhood and childcare, much of the advice was
confusing and contradictory. A very good reason has been
advanced for making a study of childcare manuals: to confine
them to their proper province by noting how their advice 'veers
with the winds of social, philosophical and psychological
change'. Such advice should therefore only be regarded as, at
best, 'a temporary crutch, not eternal verity'.[1] Just as childcare
manuals can undermine parental confidence, so too advice on
'homemaking' could and can undermine creativity and usurp
family art.

Behind much of the most impassioned advice on offer throughout the nineteenth century was a moral fervour; the family was identified as an essential bastion of society, a building block which was all the stronger for having love and morality as a principal ingredient. Perhaps nowhere was this attitude to the family thrown into sharper relief than in North America, where the home represented an outpost of order in the wilderness and a haven of serenity amid the bustle of city life.[2] This was important in itself, but by itself was not enough: the qualities fostered and conserved within the home were to flow out into society at large. 'The principle of love, which is to be carried through the universe, is first unfolded in the family', declared one American tract in mid-century.[3] Architects' and builders' manuals took up the theme:

> Home is not merely four square walls adorned with gilded pictures, but it is where love sheds its light on all the dear ones who gather round the sweet home fireside, where we can worship God, with none to molest or make us afraid.[4]

With the family having become a focus of so much expectation, the design of the home could not be left to chance. It had to make the family comfortable and secure, and to provide an environment in which family life could flourish; at the same time it was also charged with the task of symbolizing and displaying the values attached to the family. Thus for example the Gothic style might be favoured as appropriate for the house, which is also a temple of Christian values. Equally, the *inside* of the home, including its contents, was to become as loaded with meaning and moral significance as a medieval cathedral, culminating in the cultivation of the house as artistic expression in the later nineteenth century. 'The love of home is a sentiment high enough to form the nucleus of great art . . .', wrote Louis H. Gibson:

> Great architecture has always been the expression of high sentiment. . . . It must relate the love of men, women and children, youth and age. The world has never had a worthier motive for great art.[5]

Home was to be beautiful and artistic in order to provide a proper environment for personal development and the cultivation of morality. The author of *Artistic homes or how to furnish with taste* (1881) begins by stating that:

> There can be but little doubt that the surroundings of our daily life are largely instrumental, not only in affording pleasant sensations . . . but in actually moulding our natures and characters in many important respects . . .[6]

And the same book ends with a chapter which notes that:

> The introduction of illuminated text tablets as a mode of church decoration at festivals has led to a similar use of wise or pithy aphorisms as a mural adornment in our own homes . . .[7]

and proceeds to commend this practice, and to recommend the choice of mottoes

> of a character in accordance with hospitality or in grateful recognition of the Giver of all good, to whose glory, 'whether we eat or drink; or whatsoever we do', our every act should be consecrated.[8]

Not all 'art' in the home had such an overt message, but everything was chosen with care — books, pictures, ornaments, hangings — to embody and communicate values and to contribute to the home as a total environment that was also a statement capable of being read or decoded. Objects were grouped on 'what not' stands, on tables, and not least on the mantelpiece that represented the heart and hearth of the home and its essential source of comfort; poorer homes that were bare everywhere else displayed such ornaments as could be afforded on the mantelpiece. The choice was the family's; the process of choosing was a major responsibility that they could not shirk and through which they were able to express their own character and values up to a point; but the dominant values of society and the thrust and forcefulness of advice books and journals narrowed the choice considerably. Here is *Artistic homes* on the house-owners's choice of pictures:

The art treasures of his home comfort him − or his family at any rate − morning, noon, and night, they become true *lares* and *penates*, 'household gods' . . . and their influence, although silent, is very great. . . . It is precisely because things so apparently trivial as the curve of a piece of furniture, or the pattern of a wall-paper or carpet, do exert an influence more or less important on those who must pass most of their lives in gazing, consciously or not, thereon, that such things should comply with the canons of good taste. How much more important, then, that pictures should fulfil the same purpose.[9]

The reader is therefore urged to

choose art at her best, not her best only of artistic skill and technical execution, but when she stands on her highest and holiest attitudes, or paces through the grandeur or the restful calm of the visible world.[10]

Above all, those pictures which 'depict the bitter episodes of life's "seamy side"' are to be avoided at all costs. And so on. All praise then to Eliza Haweis, whose *The art of decoration* of 1881 persistently and splendidly enjoins people to 'use their own faculties, and judge for themselves what looks best here or there, and so contribute something new and individual to society';[11] advances as 'one of the first canons of good taste in house decoration . . . that our houses . . . ought to represent our individual tastes and habits, never the habits of a class';[12] asserts that 'in art matters it is better to bear with blunders of those whose taste offends you, if their taste results from thinking for themselves';[13] and insists that 'the present "aesthetic" craze unvitalized by new blood is poor and parrot-like'.[14]

Of course, the idea of the 'artistic house', the house as a kind of pedagogic museum and moral statement, merged very conveniently with self-regard and display and with a perception of house and home as a flattering reflection and outward demonstration of material success; and of course, in the capitalist ethic, material success *is* a virtue. Seen in this light, the 'artistic house' is not merely a severely limited means of genuine self-expression; it is a way of striving to conform *better* or *more*. The

32

element of display was noted by John Durand in the course of comparing American with French domestic life:

> We take delight in the reflection of ourselves in the public mirror. Self-exposure seems to us to be a matter of pride. We build our houses so that our neighbours can easily look in at the windows. We lay out our grounds and arrange our flower-beds and shrubbery expressly to be seen from the street.[15]

In England, even humble homes strove to respond to what has been called a 'consumer revolution',[16] and from as early as the eighteenth century. Without such a revolution the Industrial revolution's production of a diversity of consumer and, not least, decorative goods (pottery in Staffordshire, cutlery in Sheffield, clothing in the North West, and all manner of buttons, buckles, candlesticks, enamelware, tinware, and the like, in the Black country) could not have been sustained.

> Were an inventory to be taken of Household Goods and Furniture of a Peasant or mechanic in France, and of a Peasant or Mechanic in England, the latter would be found on average to exceed the former in value by at least three to one.

wrote Joseph Tucker, who noted such items as

> Carpets, Screens, Window Curtains, Chamber Bells, polished Brass Locks, Fenders etc. (Things hardly known abroad among persons of such rank).[17]

Through various outlets – pedlars, fairs and more and more shops – and persuaded by unprecedented marketing techniques, poorer people were offered an undreamed-of choice of cheap products and needed no persuading to imitate what they discerned to be in fashion, so that, to the horror of William Cobbett in 1825, middle-class homes formerly marked by their 'plain manners' and which had contained little other than simple, sturdy furniture, were filled with

> showy chairs . . . half-a-dozen prints in gilt frames . . . some swinging bookshelves with novels . . . many wine decanters and wine glasses . . . a dinner set . . . a breakfast set . . . desert [sic] knives . . .

and so forth. Cobbett was appalled by the 'constant anxiety to make a show'.[18] What he perhaps failed to understand was how in making a show, poorer people were reassuring themselves, clinging to visible and tangible signs of relative security. In his autobiographical *The classic slum*, Robert Roberts described how, when 'the spectre of destitution stood close', 'any new possession helped to stifle Fear'. The need for reassurance; the desire to 'show off' through the display of possessions (which perhaps amounts to no more than a way of asking for more reassurance in the form of other people's recognition of one's security and status), and a wish to enhance the pleasantness and comfort of home, mingled together:

> There was a marked division between those houses which had an overmantel and those possessing no more than a plain shelf above the fireplace. The overmantel, mirrored, and laddered with brackets, displayed a mass of tawdry ornaments, the more the better. Our own specimen the neighbours class as 'a work of art'.[19]

Even in poor homes, then, gestures were made towards the ideal of the 'artistic home'. But in such homes 'women wore their lives away' keeping dirt at bay, conjuring food and clothes from too little money, and adding, and renewing, a bare minimum of decor to the house: blacking the range, colour-stoning the doorstep and perhaps even the whole pavement 'across a width that took in one's frontage'. Again, this was partly a matter of upholding the family's image ('In a street of coloured flagstones the non-conforming housewife stood branded each week by the dirty gap before her premises') yet even as such it was inseparable from the housewife's reassuring of herself and the family that all was as well as it could be, that they were not too close to the bottom of a scale defined increasingly by the ability to consume, and which at its lower levels was an index of survival.

Thus, to the moral precepts which families were urged to observe, were increasingly added commercial pressure to *buy*; magazines combined advice and advertisements that boosted each other's function, not least when the latter appealed to the 'artistic' qualities of their commodities. ('Shopping . . . became an adventure in the high art. Department stores became museums . . .'[20]). Warnings that a preoccupation with material things could erode family virtues culminated in Veblen's coining of the phrase 'conspicuous consumption';[21] in the exposure of the fraudulent nature of the Emerald City in the *Wizard of Oz*[22] in contrast to the lasting values of a simple prairie home; and in the aesthetic reaction against clutter introduced by the Arts and Crafts Movement and taken to an extreme of austerity by Modernism.

The flood of advice and instruction, the commercial pressures, did not dry up and indeed has not done so to this day; the advice simply changed, becoming ever more contradictory as 'Modern' architects and designers in this century tried to impose an austere aesthetic that few people wanted to live in, leaving the way clear for commerce to manipulate the continuing demand for 'homely' houses and furniture, and to feed on insecurity and unconfidence by marketing tawdry imitations of, and bizarre substitutes for, the works of art, antiques and finery of the well-heeled. The result has been a perpetrating of a language of decor and artefacts in which homeliness is reduced to a set of clichés and debased symbols, and in obedience to which hard won cash — and the freedom represented by creativity — are exchanged for a 'touch of class'.[23] A happier alternative can be seen in Danish homes, for instance, which have inherited the Arts and Crafts vision of homeliness, inspired by the 'functionalism' of the traditional farmhouse rather than that of the machine, as distinct from either Victorian clutter on the one hand or the Modernist insistence that a house 'is a machine for living in' on the other, and where a dialogue involving craftsmen, designers, manufacturers, suppliers, and people at large appears not to have been fragmented to make of 'good taste' a private conversation conducted by the well-off.

I have focused on the 'artistic house', not with intent to mock but because of the ways in which it both anticipates and blocks the development of family art. The family has claimed the house as its own; it has deliberated over its decor; it has filled it to bursting with objects which speak both to the family itself, and *of* the family to the visitor. But at the same time we look in vain for private or personal references; the language of decor, of furnishing, and of ornament is a common language, evolved outside the home, determined by society and commerce, and with few, or no, words for expressing independent identities and life-styles. Even Eliza Haweis's advocacy of independence was conceived in terms of a wider choice, from the maximum extent of an existing vocabulary, as distinct from real innovation and invention. When family portraits, photographs and home-made artefacts are permitted, their existence and the ways in which they are deployed are governed by convention, as is clear from Mark Twain's inventory of an 'artistic' interior. Mark Twain has no qualms and no equal when it comes to mockery:

> Within, an uncarpeted hall, of planed boards; opening out of it, a parlor, fifteen feet by fifteen . . . ingrain carpet; mahogany center-table; lamp on it, with green paper shade — standing on a gridiron, so to speak, made of high-colored yarns, by the young ladies of the house, and called a lamp mat; several books, piled and disposed, with cast-iron exactness, according to an inherited and unchangeable plan. . . . On each end of the wooden mantel, over the fireplace, a large basket of peaches and other fruits, natural size, all done in plaster, rudely, or in wax, and painted to resemble the originals — which they don't. Over middle of mantle, engraving — Washington Crossing the Delaware; on the wall by the door, copy of it done in thunder-and-lightning crewels by one of the young ladies — work of art which would have made Washington hesitate about crossing, if he could have foreseen what advantage was going to be taken of it. Piano — kettle in disguise — with music, bound and unbound, piled on it. . . . Tilted pensively against the piano, a guitar — guitar capable of playing the Spanish fandango by itself, if you give it a start. Frantic work of art on the wall — pious motto, done on the premises, sometimes in colored yarns, sometimes in faded grasses: progenitor of the 'God Bless Our Home' of modern commerce. Framed in black moldings on the wall, other works of art, conceived and committed on the premises, by the young ladies; being grim black-and-white crayons; landscapes, mostly: lake, solitary sailboat, petrified clouds, pre-geological trees on

shore, anthracite precipice; name of criminal conspicuous in the corner. Lithograph, Napoleon Crossing the Alps. Lithograph, The Grave at St. Helena. Steel plates, Trumbull's Battle of Bunker Hill, and the Sally from Gibraltar. Copperplates, Moses Smiting the Rock, and Return of the Prodigal Son. In big gilt frame, slander of the family in oil: papa holding a book ('Constitution of the United States'); guitar leaning against Mama, blue ribbons fluttering from its neck; the young ladies, as children, in slippers and scalloped pantalettes, one embracing toy horse, the other beguiling kitten with ball of yarn, and both simpering up at Mama, who simpers back. These persons all fresh, raw, and red — apparently skinned. Opposite, in gilt frame, grandpa and grandma, at thirty and twenty-two, stiff, old-fashioned, high-collared, puff-sleeved, glaring pallidly out from a background of solid Egyptian night. Under a glass French clock dome, large bouquet of stiff flowers done in corpsy white wax. Pyramidal whatnot in the corner, the shelves occupied chiefly with bric-a-brac of the period; disposed with an eye to best effect: shell, with the Lord's Prayer carved on it; another shell — of the long-oval sort, narrow, straight orifice, three inches long, running from end to end — portrait of Washington carved on it; not well done; the shell had Washington's mouth, originally — artist should have built to that. These two are memorials of the long-ago bridal trip to New Orleans and the French Market. Other bric-a-brac: Californian 'specimens' — quartz, with gold wart adhering; old Guinea-gold locket, with circlet of ancestral hair in it; Indian arrowheads, of flint; pair of bead moccasins, from uncle who crossed the Plains; three 'alum' baskets of various colors — being skeleton frame of wire, clothed-on with cubes of crystallized alum in the rock-candy style — works of art which were achieved by the young ladies; their doubles and duplicates to be found upon all whatnots in the land; convention of dessicated bugs and butterflies pinned to a card; painted toy dog, seated upon bellows attachment — drops its under jaw and squeaks when pressed upon; sugar-candy rabbit — limbs and features merged together, not strongly defined; pewter presidential campaign medal; miniature cardboard wood sawyer, to be attached to the stovepipe and operated by the heat; small Napoleon done in wax; spread-open daguerreotypes of dim children, parents, cousins, aunts and friends, in all attitudes but customary ones; no templed portico

37

at back, and manufactured landscape stretching away in the distance — that came in later, with the photograph; all these vague figures lavishly chained and ringed — metal indicated and secured from doubt by stripes and splashes of vivid gold bronze; all of them too much combed, too much fixed up; and all of them uncomfortable in inflexible Sunday clothes of a pattern which the spectator cannot realize could ever have been in fashion; husband and wife generally grouped together — husband sitting, wife standing, with hand on his shoulder — and both preserving, all these fading years, some traceable effect of the daguerreotypist's brisk 'Now smile, if you please!' Bracketed over whatnot — place of special sacredness — an outrage in watercolor, done by the young niece that came on a visit long ago, and died. Pity, too; for she might have repented of this in time. Horsehair chairs, horsehair sofa which keeps sliding from under you. Window shades, of oil stuff, with milkmaids and ruined castles stenciled on them in fierce colors. Lambrequins dependant from gaudy boxings of beaten tin, gilded.[24]

One development should not be overlooked: a room of one's own. Private rooms for members of the family developed in part as a response to the restlessness of older children who might otherwise be tempted away from home by new opportunities.

> Without it (one's own room) it is only their father's home, not theirs. But, by giving them their own apartment, they themselves become personally identified with it, and hence love to adorn and perfect all parts.[25]

Private rooms in the further recesses of the house, which would seldom if ever be penetrated by anyone from outside the family, eased the pressure to conform and facilitated the growth of more individual attitudes to the house and to personal possessions. This is beautifully expressed by Jane Austen in *Mansfield Park*. Fanny has a room she can go to

> after anything unpleasant below, and find immediate consolation in some pursuit, or some train of thought at hand. Her plants, her books . . . her writing desk, and her works of charity and ingenuity, were all within her reach; or if indisposed for employment, if nothing but musing would do, she could scarcely

see an object in that room which had not an interesting remembrance connected with it.[26]

Here is a different approach to possessions, one of valuing them not for their moral lessons or material worth but above all for their personal association, their ability to trigger memories, to become vessels of personal knowledge and experience, to reflect and confirm identity. It is in this sense that Fanny's room is a 'nest of comforts'.

In his marvellous and important book *A pattern language*, the architect Christopher Alexander offers an alternative to, and a critique of, 'homemaking'. His overall aim is, not to dispense conventional advice but to restore to people the confidence and ability to take an active part in shaping their own habitat in their own way. The very last section is entitled 'Things from your life'. He begins:

> 'Decor' and the conception of 'interior design' have spread so widely, that very often people forget their instinct for the things they really want to keep around them.

And he goes on:

> It is obvious that the things around you should be the things which mean most to you, which have the power to play a part in the continuous process of self-transformation which is your life. . . . But this function has eroded, gradually, in modern times because people have begun to look outward, to others, and over their shoulders, at the people who are coming to visit them, and have replaced their natural instinctive decorations with the things which they believe will please and impress their visitors. This is the motive behind all the interior design and decor in the women's magazines. And designers play on these anxieties . . .
>
> But the irony is, that the visitors who come into a room don't want this nonsense any more than the people who live there. It is far more fascinating to come into a room which is the living expression of a person, or a group of people, so that you can see their lives, their inclinations, displayed in manifest form around the walls, in the furniture, on the shelves.

His advice takes us to the heart of the subject of *this* book:

> Do not be tricked into believing that modern decor must be slick or psychedelic, or 'natural' or 'modern art', or 'plants' or anything else that current taste-makers claim. It is most beautiful when it comes straight from your life — the things you care for, the things that tell your story.[27]

4

A 'Labour of Love'

To whom should we so confidently apply for all that concerns
the beautifying of home-life as to the presiding spirit of the
home? Why should not the instinctive taste and natural grace of
woman be reflected in the hues and harmonies of colour and
form on the walls of her rooms, on the curtains arranged by her
deft fingers, on the soft carpet beneath her feet, and in the
thousand forms of comfort, convenience, or elegance which
surround her?

'Art-work for Women I', *Art Journal*, 1872

Much of the literature on 'homemaking' (like that on childcare)
was either addressed directly to women, or defined, elevated,
yet confined woman's role by designating her 'the presiding
spirit of home'. 'It is the province of woman to make home',
wrote one gentleman in 1837; 'If she makes that delightful and
salutary — the abode of order and purity, though she may
never herself step beyond the threshold, she may yet send
forthe from her humble dwelling, a power that will be felt
round the globe.'[1] Such was the role propagated for women by
men and women too, accepted or absorbed into their way of life
by many housewives. It was a role which, in particular, both
lauded, and *limited*, female creativity, smothering it with advice
and instruction as well as restriction; yet creativity could win
through, sometimes in open rebellion, sometimes through
covert expression of frustration, and sometimes — as we shall
see — by bringing to 'homemaking' a truly innovative spirit,

41

transforming it by making of it a 'labour of love', and by winning from it family art.

A book like this cannot hope to do justice to the history of woman as housewife or of the ways in which men have taken unfair advantage of what biology has determined: that women are child-bearers and nurturers. What is of particular interest in relation to family art is the ideal of woman as homemaker and mistress of arts (or crafts) which was grafted onto the housewifely role. From the fifteenth century, when Mary and the female saints began to be depicted as gentler and more maternal than their queenly and aristocratic bearing in medieval iconography, as befitted the relatively domestic settings in which they now appeared, a clear division opened between professional embroidery and the activities of women in the home who were responsible for an 'extraordinary spread of domestic embroidery':

> Every conceivable surface became a site for embroidery: sheets, valances and coverlets, table carpets, cupboard carpets, cushion for benches and chairs, coifs, stomachers, sleeves, handker-chiefs, bags, hawking gear, needlecases, book covers, book marks, book cushions, shoes, gloves and aprons.[2]

Embroidery became part of a woman's education, if that can possibly be the right word for a strictly limited, vocational training for a lifelong occupation; as such, and because of its domestic applications, it was downgraded to a mere 'craft' among the arts. Thus Nicholas Hilliard in *A treatise concerning the art of limning* of c.1600 carefully and deliberately distinguished painting by *dis*association:

> It tendeth not to common men's use, either for furnishing houses or any patterns for tapestries.

In the seventeenth century Dutch town house, the physical separation of (male) 'work' from the home, and a very modest use of servants, consolidated and enhanced the responsibilities of married women who had 'the whole care and absolute management of all their Domestique'; paintings of Dutch interiors made this housewifely role visible in such a way as to make it seem timeless and inevitable. In painting after painting we see a wife, or a wife and a servant, putting away clean linen, sweeping the floor, bent over needlework, or playing a musical instrument.

But it was with the nineteenth century and the ideal of the 'artistic house' in particular, that a powerful image of the housewife as a mistress of arts was created, its roots in historical precedent imaginatively enriched — Roszika Parker has shown how an idea of the medieval noblewoman, chastely and patiently embroidering in her secluded rooms in the safety of the castle, became a 'blue-print for the middle-class Victorian wife . . .'[3] Woman as 'presiding spirit' of the home needed to be equipped with an array of skills, including needlework which

> brings daily blessings to every home, unnoticed, perhaps, because of its hourly silent application; for in a household each stitch is one for comfort to some person or other and without its ever watchful care home would be a scene of discomfort indeed.[4]

To support this womanly role, the literature of 'homemaking' was expanded to include 'how to' and 'hobby' books; magazines provided patterns for needlework from the late eighteenth century; suppliers marketed materials, kits, and patterns. Indeed, this is still the case:

> 'Knit his 'n hers sweaters', 'A pretty layette for baby' and 'Bean bags for the boys' are typical titles of craft projects to be found in women's magazines which serve to reproduce and support the 'norm' of the nuclear family unit and the place and function of woman within it.[5]

Not only is there nothing creative about slavishly following patterns, but ill-conceived projects, promoted as part of an urging of the housewife to make, make, make, have yielded some dire results, provoking Charles Kingsley, for instance, to speak of 'the abomination of "Fancy work" . . .'[6] But at the same time we should beware of identifying creativity purely and simply with extrovert self-expression or 'originality'. Folk art produced subtle variations on established themes:

43

. . . Quilt patterns were published and passed along in the 19th century (just as fashionable art styles are in today's art world). The innovative quilt maker or group of makers would come up with a new idea that broke or enriched the rules, just as the Navajo rug maker might vary brilliantly within set patterns (and modern abstractionists innovate by sticking to the rules of innovation).

Just so:

> The shared or published pattern forms the same kind of armature . . . for freedom of expression within a framework as the underlying grid does in contemporary painting.[7]

And indeed it is right and proper that quilting, embroidery, and other products of women's creativity in the home have been subject to reassessment, by feminist art historians in particular, and have inspired, and been celebrated by, some contemporary women artists.[8] Miriam Schapiro, for instance, has made artworks from scraps of material like those to be found in a thrifty housewife's rag-bag, cutting out and incorporating patchwork shapes of a heart and a house, in conscious tribute to her own mother's 'labour of love'.

'Homemaking' defined women's creativity in a way that limited it from the outset; it also added to the burden of housework. The effect this could have on a woman's innate creativity is movingly and illuminatingly told by a nineteenth century American housewife, Jane Swisshelm:

> During all my girlhood I saw no pictures, no art gallery, no studio, but had learned to feel great contempt for my own efforts at picture-making. A traveling artist stopped in Wilkinsburg and painted some portraits; we visited his studio, and a new world opened to me. Up to that time painting had seemed as inaccessible as the moon − a sublimity I no more thought of reaching than a star; but when I saw a portrait on the easel, a palette of paints and some brushes, I was at home in a new world . . .
>   Bard, the wagon-maker, made me a stretcher, and with a yard of unbleached muslin, some tacks and white lead, I made a

canvas. In the shop were white lead, lampblack, king's yellow and red lead, with oil and turpentine. I watched Bard mix paints, and concluded I wanted brown. Years before, I heard of brown umber, so I got umber and some brushes and began my husband's portrait. I hid it when he was there or I heard any one coming, and once blistered it badly trying to dry it before the fire, so that it was a very rough work; but it was a portrait, a daub, a likeness, and the hand was his hand and no other. The figure was correct, and the position in the chair, and, from the moment I began it, I felt I had found my vocation . . . I forgot God, and did not know it; forgot philosophy, and did not care to remember it; but alas! I forgot to get Bard's dinner, and, although I forgot to be hungry, I had no reason to suppose he did. He would willingly have gone hungry, rather than give any one trouble; but I had neglected a duty. Not only once did I do this; but again and again, the fire went out or the bread ran over in the pans, while I painted and dreamed.

My conscience began to trouble me. Housekeeping was 'woman's sphere', although I had never then heard the words, for no woman had gotten out of it to be hounded back; but I knew my place and scorned to leave it. I tried to think I could paint without neglect of duty. It did not occur to me that painting was a duty for a married woman! Had the passion seized me before marriage, no other love could have come between me and art; but I felt that it was too late, as my life was already devoted to another subject – housekeeping.

It was a hard struggle. I tried to compromise, but experience soon deprived me of that hope, for to paint was to be oblivious of all other things. In my doubt, I met one of those newspaper paragraphs with which men are wont to pelt women into subjection: 'A man does not marry an artist, but a housekeeper'. This fitted my case, and my doom was sealed.

I put away my brushes; resolutely crucified my divine gift, and while it hung writhing on the cross, spent my best years and powers cooking cabbage . . .[9]

It is noteworthy that Jane began by painting a portrait of her husband – family art that ought to be reconcileable with housekeeping. But Jane's creative impulse could not easily submit to restraint; clearly she was a born artist who should have had the opportunity to explore and develop her gift as freely as any man. When such opportunities were at last granted to women, they came, significantly, in the area of craft and design education in the first instance, and only later in the 'fine' arts; initially conceived as an extension of the educating of women as homemakers, and of the tuition which better-off families had been able to buy in for their daughters, art school classes for women were presented conservatively:

> We may remark, at the risk of repetition, that there is here no question of the introduction of women to new employments, or of the danger of tempting them from their homes.[10]

Yet many women have somehow been able to reconcile their innate creativity with a domestic role, sometimes happily, sometimes with mixed feelings but in ways which, rather than confronting domesticity head-on, transform it more or less successfully into a 'labour of love'. Just how much of a woman, and of a family, could be stitched into a quilt, even into a geometric design that on the face of it does not give anything away, is revealed in this recollection:

> It took me nearly twenty years, nearly twenty-five, I reckon, in the evening after supper when the children were all put to bed. My whole life is in that quilt. It scares me sometimes when I look at it. All my joys and all my sorrows are stitched into those little pieces. When I was proud of the boys and when I was downright provoked and angry with them. When the girls annoyed me or when they gave me a warm feeling around my heart. And John too. He was stitched into that quilt and all the thirty years we were married. Sometimes I loved him and sometimes I sat there hating him as I pieced the patches together. So they are all in that quilt, my hopes and fears, my joys and sorrows, my loves and hates. I tremble sometimes when I remember what that quilt knows about me.[11]

Such a quilt is an example of what Melissa Meyer and Miriam Schapiro have called 'femmage' — a collage-like reassembling of bits and pieces, inspired or necessitated by a thrifty using of what is to hand and might otherwise be wasted.[12] 'Necessity is the mother, not the father of invention', says Lucy Lippard.[13] And indeed the very materials available inspired innovation, where a kit would have produced imitation; not only that, but their associations — the fact that, as dresses, shirts, curtains, or whatever, the scraps of material had already been part of the family's visual world and might be identified with particular members of the family — made of their reassembly the creating of a special kind of family chronicle and archive, an embellishing of home with memories of itself.

The improvising of various artefacts, from bits and pieces, was often praised as 'making something from nothing', but did not invariably demonstrate the miracle of creativity which that phrase suggests. However, Robert Roberts' tribute to his mother, who had poverty and a husband prone to drunkenness to contend with in the insalubrious environment of the Salford slums, bears eloquent witness to motherhood at its most creative:

> Skill seemed to flow through my mother's fingers. . . . My sisters said she could stare a few minutes at any garment in a shop window, then come home and make a replica. Did I, or another child, catch her at ease and want a kite that flew, a castle from a sauce box, a bow that really shot arrows? She turned them out, and well . . .[14]

Where imitation was required, she achieved it without help from a pattern or kit; given a free hand, she didn't hesitate to originate and invent. The creativity which childcare requires, and that children themselves can inspire, sometimes doesn't call for more than perceiving a possibility and allowing it to happen. Such an incident was recorded by Mrs Almira Phelps in a diary of observations of her own child in the 1830s. She gave her boy a box of wafers and let him shake and pull at the box until he was able to open it. When 'hundreds of bright round pieces fell about him in glorious confusion' she felt that he 'had conquered a difficulty and had made a discovery'.[15] Undoubtedly *my* mother's creativity, including her activities as an amateur artist (and a willingness to let things happen — as I write this I suddenly and vividly recall free-ranging explorations and tippings-out of her bag of assorted buttons), account for my becoming interested in art at an early age, while sadly and ironically my interest in art certainly contributed to my becoming a harsh judge of much of what she actually produced. At the same time I detected, and reacted against, the 'stink of poverty'[16] associated with the necessarily homemade – money was short, and we often had to 'make do'; the results seemed a poor substitute for what money could buy. (Happily, what I regard as by far my mother's best painting is a portrait of our eldest son, done from a photograph recording a memorable occasion – a notable example of family art.)

In sometimes 'making something from nothing', or allowing marvels to happen as if out of nothing, Woman continues an ancient tradition, of priestess, mediator between Nature and Man; she re-enacts a revelation, teaches how to see by showing what is there to be seen, in a context in which

> the idea is no longer to make nothings into somethings, but to transform and give meanings to all things.[17]

Something of this same role comes into play in her involvement, as 'presiding spirit' and tutelar, in breadmaking, the preparation of food, the ceremonies which attend its eating and which bless the house:

> It is easy to make of love
> these ceremonials. As priests
> we fold cloth, break bread, share wine,
> hope there's enough to go round.[18]

Yet what is being referred to here is surely a 'femininity' that women and men share, if not in equal part?

Family art, as we will discover, is a particular way of giving 'meaning to things'; as such it has a universal significance beyond superficial gender roles and stereotypes. It, and families, can only gain from a freeing of the 'housewife' from drudgery and confinement, and, too, from a liberating of men *into* the family, willing and unabashed in their commitment of more of their time, their skill, and themselves to family and home. But at the same time the women demonstrating for

48

peace at Greenham Common air base from 1982, hardened 'liberated' protesters, knew well that an all-woman protest would be different in kind from one in which women and men joined together, and it is still hard to imagine that anyone other than women, at that moment in history, could have fixed baby clothes, a wedding dress, and family photographs, to the wire fence of the base, risking sentimentality, movingly deploying symbols of family love against the nightmare of nuclear war.

The achievement of the Greenham women affirms Caroline Hill's tentative answer to her own question that she posed over 80 years ago and that highlights a larger theme of the present book:

> Should women be educated for the world or for the one career of homemaking? The solution is easier if the world is looked upon as the home.[19]

5

At Home with the Larssons

There could be no more complete example of family art than the home which Carl and Karin Larsson created at Sundborn, in Sweden, at the turn of the century: a home which, incorporating family portraits, inspired in part by folk art, an inspiration for a series of books which extend the literature of 'homemaking', and the work of husband and wife together but not least of the wife, represents a culmination of developments we have noted in the first part of this book, and illustrates all the aspects and qualities of family art that will be explored in the chapters that follow.

Carl Larsson and Karin Bergöö married in 1883. Both were Swedish artists, living and working as members of the artists' colony at Grèz, near Barbizon, in France. Carl Larsson had had an unhappy childhood in a Stockholm slum, had entered Stockholm's Royal Academy of Fine Arts at the early age of thirteen, and had worked as a retoucher of photographs, an illustrator and a reporter, but it was in the open air at Grèz that he began to find his way as a painter after a period of struggle and depression. Karin was the daughter of a wealthy merchant family; her parents had recognized and encouraged her artistic talents, and she too had studied at the Royal Academy of Fine Arts, and subsequently, at the Academie Colarossi in Paris. At Grèz, Larsson set up his easel next to hers; in a posthumous autobiography he later acknowledged how painting with Karin had helped him to become a different artist, whereas Karin gained from him a new confidence. 'Previously I never thought

I would come to play any role in this life. I thought I was merely a subordinate character, that I was made to serve as a background for other characters, so that they could be better seen', she wrote to her parents. Yet Larsson shared the then still common view that a woman's place was in the home, to the extent of opposing the admission of women to academic artistic training. Soon after their marriage, Karin stopped painting and instead confined her creativity to the home; but there it flourished, contributing to the transformation of the home and finding expression in particular in Karin's considerable achievement as a textile artist. And Karin and Carl Larsson's creating of their home was to give Carl Larsson the subject matter which, as an artist, he would excel in above all else, for at Karin's suggestion he produced many pictures of their home and family life.

The Larssons returned to Sweden in 1885, settling initially in Stockholm before moving to Gothenburg the next year, and then returning to the capital in 1893 where Carl Larsson, now an established artist, began work on a series of murals at the Nationalmuseum. Meanwhile in 1888 Karin's father gave them the cottage at Sundborn that they used first as a summer house, and then as a permanent residence from 1901, extending the original building as their family grew. There were to be seven children altogether, Suzanne, Ulf, Pontus, Lisbeth, Brita, Kersti, and Esbjörn. Adding to their property at Sundborn, the family ran a small farm including seven cows and two horses, in so doing consciously putting down roots in Nature and identifying themselves with the rural community in which traditional folk art and a range of crafts still flourished. Local craftsmen were employed to assist in the continual process of enlarging and fitting-out the house; Carl Larsson recalled how:

> off and on, and with small extra savings, Karin and I, with the help of the village carpenters, blacksmith, bricklayer, and painter, did it up, a bit here, and a bit there.

And in 1912 the family bought, at a nearby village, and re-assembled as another extension to the house, an old log cabin decorated with traditional paintings.

51

Folk art, then, was one of the Larssons' sources of inspiration; another was the Arts and Crafts Movement that was in part a reaction against the over-cluttered 'artistic home' and which emphasized instead honest craftsmanship and simple, integrated interior design. But in the context of this book in particular, what is so special about the Larsson home is, first, that its uncluttered, light interiors clearly provided an excellent environment for family life, and secondly, that in banishing clutter the Larssons created space in which to weave their family life and identity into the very fabric of the house. Thus, rather than proclaiming the family's moral fibre, social status, or superior taste, the message of the house, to family and visitors was, simply, 'This is *our* home'.

For what is extraordinary about the Larsson home, what cannot be accounted for in terms of external influence, is its wealth of personal, familial references. For instance, a dedication to Karin is included in the border that Carl Larsson painted around the door of her room; another door, elsewhere in the house, originally carried a portrait of Karin on its lower panel while higher up it bore an inscription, in English, adapted from a verse by Kate Greenaway:

> There was a little woman
> Lived with CL
> And if she is not gone
> She lives there still –
> very well.

Another portrait of Karin fills a panel in the door of the 'workshop' (the original studio). A full-length portrait of Kersti in a red dress, against a red and white chequered background, occupies a panel on the inside of the door into the library. A delightful full-length portrait of Brita, wearing a nightdress embroidered with her initials, is framed in the central panel of a

Plate 5 (opposite) *Suzanne, Ulf, Pontus, Lisbeth, June 1891.* Carl Larsson. Ink on paper. (Collection: Albert Bonniers Förlag AB, Stockholm, Sweden) This drawing records one of the first wall decorations that Larsson made in the house at Sundborn.

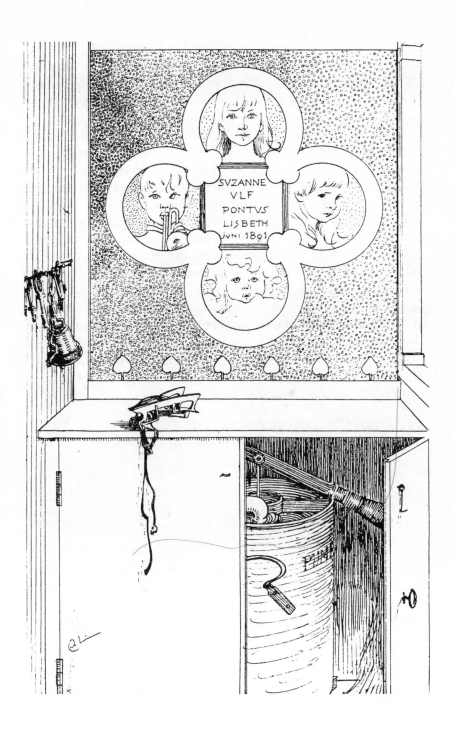

large seventeenth-century cupboard; the cupboard is dated 1694, the portrait, 1897. An older Brita gazes out from yet another door panel. Esbjörn also has a door panel to himself. A mural portrays the faces of each of the then four children, in roundels, with their names – Suzanne, Ulf, Pontus, Lisbeth – and the date – 'Juni 1891' – in the centre. Carl and Karin's initials were included by Karin in a woven table covering. And so on. Such details are evidence of an independence from prevailing conventions, which freed the Larssons to make their home in response to their own needs and wishes; to 'blend the old and the new, things foreign and Swedish, expensive and cheap',[1] according to their own choice; to create rooms, and to design and make, or to design and commission, furniture, to suit themselves and their children. Throughout, but most splendidly of all in Carl Larsson's bedroom (where the curtained bed is a room within the room), the house is enriched and softened by curtains, drapes, blankets, table- and floor-coverings woven by Karin, which no words of mine can do justice to either as individual pieces or in their cumulative effect. Such a home both housed and reflected its family as completely, as comfortingly, as a house could.

Fiona MacCarthy has written of how those involved in the Arts and Crafts Movement were 'attuned to ceremony':

> not the pompous worldly ceremonial – this they detested – but the private ceremony, the marking of occasions; and the family ceremonies in many households, the mealtimes, birthdays, comings-of-age, Christmases and weddings, were in themselves made strong artistic statements, living art.[2]

The Larsson home – which Carl Larsson referred to as a 'work of all arts' – was a theatre of family life and of family ceremonies enacted as 'living art'. Several of these are illustrated in Carl Larsson's paintings, of which one in particular depicts a Name Day morning in the Larsson household. The other children have evidently crept out of bed as quietly as mice, and have now dressed up to wake the one whose Name Day it is with coffee in bed; a neighbour provides music on his

Plate 6 'A Day of Celebration'. Carl Larsson. Watercolour 32×43 cm. (Nationalmuseum, Stockholm. Photo: Statens Konstmuseer)

violin; a poem has been composed and is about to be read from a scroll; an initial and a heart have been made from flowers wound onto a wire frame. Here in a single image is family art complete – in the room itself, designed and decorated by the Larssons; in the ceremony and its ingredients that include elements of music, literature, and theatre; and finally, in Carl's recording of all of this in a painting that can be likened to a family snapshot.

In fact Carl Larsson's paintings of home and family were painted primarily to be published, in a series of books beginning with *Ett hem* ('A home') in 1899.[3] Interestingly, these books are related to the literature of 'homemaking'; through the books, the Larssons rather tentatively offered their home as a source of inspiration. Carl Larsson's preface to *Ett hem* struck a hesitant, almost apologetic note when he explained how he felt the Larsson house

can serve as – dare I stand up and say it – as an example – there now, I've said it – for many persons who feel a need to arrange their home in a pleasant manner.

Rather than using the text to set himself up either as a moral authority or as an arbiter of taste, Carl Larsson employed words lightly and anecdotally, as an embellishment of the pictures and to help them to help the house tell one family's story in a way which other families were left free to respond to as they wished. Moreover, and remarkably, the pictures themselves do not illustrate an uninhabited 'model' house; even where rooms are shown without people, there are invariably signs that people are not far away, have perhaps just gone out and will soon return – knitting that has only recently been put down; a newspaper, slippers, a pipe and a book, left none too tidily on a settee and outlining the shape of a contented and comfortable father like a hare's form. Often someone's presence is partially revealed, or is glimpsed through an open door. But in many cases the rooms are very definitely inhabited: in some cases they are the scene of a significant moment in the family's history, like the Name Day ceremony described above; in others, we find ourselves observing unexceptional everyday activities.

Thus, as well as contributing in an original and even revolutionary way to the literature of 'homemaking', Carl Larsson's watercolours belong firmly in the tradition of 'conversation pieces', those paintings of inhabited, informal domestic interiors which we glanced at in an earlier chapter. Carl Larsson was of course aware of this tradition, and a framed engraving of an eighteenth-century example of the genre, by Greuze, can be seen hanging on the wall in one of the pictures in *Ett hem*. But also, Carl Larsson's pictures, and the way in which he gathered them into books, do comprise a family album and anticipate ways in which many families have used photography.

Like any other family album, Carl Larsson's paintings reflect, principally, domestic harmony. He chose to capture 'the happy and charming scenes which are played all the time under my eyes'; he perhaps went further than some of us would in recording occasions of the kind that might be laughed at afterwards but were less than blissful at the time – a naughty child dismissed from the supper table and made to wait in the corner, 'Sjusoverskans dystra frukost' ('Lie-abeds sad breakfast'), or heads bent unenthusiastically over homework. Sickness is not excluded: 'Konvalescens' depicts Karin on her sickbed, recuperating from a serious attack of pneumonia. But every family has somehow to cope with *dis*harmony; in an oil painting, 'Nu är det jul igen' ('Now it's Christmas again') of 1907, Carl Larsson portrays himself staring moodily out of the window, half-turned away from the crowd of revellers in his own home, as if unable to enter into the spirit of the occasion. (Or is this his way of representing his involvement in a scene in which, as its *witness*, he could not at that moment have been in the centre of?)

Carl Larsson was in fact a complex character, for whom the attainment of domestic happiness and of artistic success were achievements that he could never take for granted, lifelines for one who had surfaced, struggling, from a miserable childhood.

If he felt guilt at having confined Karin to a domestic role, it has been suggested that he 'sometimes also felt imprisoned by her';[4] if, in suggesting that he paint his domestic scenes, Karin had led him to what, perhaps, he could do best of all, he never gave up ambitions to be more than a painter of domesticity. On the one hand, paintings of home confined *his* creativity to the home *too*; on the other, the work he did outside the home, and on a grand scale, did not, finally, win the acclaim he yearned for: some later murals for the Nationalmuseum provoked a highly critical response and were eventually rejected. Yet Carl's deepest feelings towards Karin were surely expressed in his references to her as the 'good angel' of his life, which found visual expression in one extraordinary watercolour — extra-ordinary, because in every other respect it is, so to speak, just another painting of a room in the Larsson home, a celebration of ordinariness. 'Hemmets goda ängel' ('Home's good angel') of 1909 depicts a mysterious ethereal female figure in a sunlit bedroom which Carl had decorated as a gift for Karin to mark her Name Day in 1894. A lapse into sentimentality it may be; yet I do not believe it should be dismissed as, simply, another invocation of the nineteenth century ideal of femininity. Carl Larsson was not, after all, a husband who took his ease while his wife made a comfortable home around him; rejoicing and participating in the comprehensive transformation of his and their home, he was intimately involved in a creative partnership with its 'presiding spirit'.

There is one more thing to be said about the Larssons 'at home' that has a bearing on the nature of family art. Carl Larsson's picture books, I suggest, represent a remarkable extending of hospitality; they are a family album which the reader is invited to browse through, and Carl's text says exactly the kind of thing he would be likely to say if he was standing at the reader's elbow; through the pictures we are invited to enter the home and share in family life. That the Larssons were hospitable is apparent from many of the pictures, such as the one that shows guests at a Christmas party, referred to above; a sense of, almost, an extended family is conveyed by the quite frequent appearance of neighbours, of local craftsmen working on the house, of Carl's models, of the family servant. One special guest, Carl's friend Prince Eugen, himself an artist, was the subject and recipient of a watercolour showing his being woken in the morning by two of the girls bearing candles: a glimpse of a choir singing outside may have been a conceit but on the other hand is just the kind of impromptu ceremony Carl and Karin were capable of organizing with the help of their friends. As a work of family art — a 'work of arts' indeed — the Larsson home at Sundborn is the more complete because it is an open house; the decoration of the front door with a message of welcome from Carl and Karin Larsson is crucial, not an afterthought.

6

Mirrors and Memories

Photographs, said Oliver Wendell Holmes, are 'mirrors with memories', reflections frozen in time. The social history of the mirror and its role in the development of human consciousness and civilization has yet to be written. In mirrors we see ourselves, with astonishing clarity; mirrors confirm our identity and tell us that we are and who we are. Thus it seems reasonable to suppose that the increasing availability of mirrors from the Middle Ages must have contributed to the development of more self-conscious and reflective attitudes. (In seventeenth-century Holland, breaking a mirror was regarded as a sign of an approaching death, the fragmenting of an identity. After death, mirrors − and pictures − were turned to face the wall. Even today, we still speak of the breaking of a mirror as heralding 7 years' bad luck.)

Prior to the development of photography, painted portraits, as well as mirrors (which were often similarly framed) introduced personal likenesses as features of the home; paintings portrayed individuals and families in formal poses and later, informally, in 'conversation pieces'. If these anticipated family snapshots, the services offered by less distinguished portrait painters to the not so well-off anticipated those provided by photographers, and miniature paintings and cut-out silhouettes foreshadowed the use of small photographs of loved ones that we have become accustomed to carrying with us in wallets, pocket-books, and suitcases. Framed photographs congregated on mantelpieces, a miniature portrait gallery at the heart of the home; in the Larsson home, in addition to the unprecedented way in which images of members of the family were incorporated in the decor, a special corner was set aside for a display of photographs of ancestors and of cherished objects (notably a bowl used for the christening of all the children on a single, memorable occasion). Thus home became a world of mirrors, in which individual family members continually glimpsed their own reflection; or rather, the whole house was made into a single, faceted mirror that reflected the identity of the family as a whole, and of individuals as members of the household. This chapter will examine the role of likenesses as mirrors with memories, and of objects that mirror or represent personal or familial identity, in making home an environment that constantly confirms a family's corporate identity (death notwithstanding) and mutual affection.

Not everyone had been able to afford painted portraits; few people had the confidence and skill to paint their own. With the invention of photography, portraits of family groups and of individual members of the family became easier and cheaper to obtain through a visit to a photographer's studio, for instance; in addition, some photographers wandered the streets offering their services or taking speculative shots of children in the hope of selling prints to the parents. It is known that this happened even in poor areas of Manchester, where families would pose in front of their terraced houses.[1] With the development of simple cameras, and of roll film and film processing services, photography, as a means of making one's own pictures, became available to many more people who needed neither wealth nor skill.[2] From the beginning, Kodak's advertising of the Brownie promoted its use for family pictures, and in particular for informal 'snapshots'. 'Snaps' took their place alongside formal portraits in the family album, and on the mantelpiece, and then largely took over but for the occasional school or team photograph. The family album (subject of the next chapter) became a prime means for every family to record, remember, and browse over its activities.

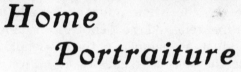

KODAK

Home
Portraiture

It is simpler than most people think.
Beautiful results are obtained by the
light of an ordinary window or by flash-
light.

Plate 7 An early Kodak advertisement and (opposite) a Kodak film
wallet.

Kodak
Film Wallet

J. BURY Ltd.,
E. S. BURY, M.P.S.,
Homœopathic & Dispensing Chemists,
5, ST. ANN STREET,
MANCHESTER.

But the idea of the mirror – or rather, of *reflections* – can be taken further. The content of some portraits and photographs gives a clue – sometimes the portrayal is enhanced by the inclusion of objects of which the sitter is particularly fond, or by portraying people in their favourite surroundings: the family in its home, for example. In these cases, objects and surroundings tell us more about the person or persons than their mere appearance, and thus enrich the likeness.

Objects and likenesses, photographs and things, complement each other in other ways too. A family album compiled to record a holiday might include in it not only snapshots, but also, picture-postcards, bus tickets, luggage labels, hotel bills, menus, and other ephemeral items that are the touchstones of memories. Other souvenirs, from stones and shells from the beach to a 'plastic Eiffel tower',[3] are likely to be brought back and displayed in the home; there they join other keepsakes, among the family photos, pictures on the wall, familiar furniture: images and objects together form a total environment, a single created work, never complete, which the family extends into the future and with which it embraces its past. Collecting − not for investment, or for the sake of hoarding, or for purely aesthetic or other reasons, but simply because wherever a family goes things attach themselves to it; because its members gather or give to one another tokens of shared experience and interests; because things are garnered in and given a place in the home − for these reasons, collecting and selecting can be a feature of family art. And so it becomes clear that questions of 'beauty' or 'taste', whereas not unimportant (who would not surround themselves and their children, so far as they are able, with what they conceive to be beautiful?) are not crucial to the primary role of family art.

> The aesthete can call the plastic Eiffel tower on the shelves as awful as he wishes. But has he any knowledge of the happy memories which are bound up with this little souvenir? The plastic tower may have the same place in the life of the family as Rembrandt's 'Jewish Bride' has in European art'[4]

Whereas likenesses reflect our appearance, things can become almost part of us, and thus may reflect some aspect of us. Clearly, this has little to do simply with acquisition and possession; it has everything to do with familiarity and use. We do not enlarge our personalities by acquiring more and more things, but things that we identify with, including things we use (and that extend our capabilities) and things that we cherish, and not least, things we make ourselves, become, for us and for those close to us, a part of us that may outlast us. Objects, a favourite chair, a room, the home, are in this sense like the clothes we wear; our clothes not least are likely to remain identified with us after we outgrow them − and even after death.

In the home, likenesses and objects reflect individuals within the context of the family and household, a community of people and things; home, and family art, tell us not only who we are, but where and among whom we belong. Whereas particular likenesses reflect the family at a point in time, family art as a continuing process grows with the family: the family album accumulates, the house is extended. Family art accompanies the family into the future, but in doing so it brings the past with it. In particular, it ensures that deceased members of the family are not forgotten, by preserving their memory, and their likeness, to the point of denying death its victory. In many family portraits, members of the family were painted together with sublime disregard of mortality, and in a way that perhaps bears comparison with the instinct to leave certain possessions, or a particular room, undisturbed for years after the death of their owner. Ways of remembering the dead — of, almost, re-incorporating them into the living family, through both likenesses and objects — add an important dimension to family art.

The dead were painted among the living; the living were sometimes painted holding, or looking at, or sitting or standing near, previously executed portraits of the dead. Likenesses of the recently deceased — and of the living with an emphasis on the fact that they would one day be dead — were a stock-in-trade of both painters and early photographers. American portrait painters advertised their willingness to paint portraits, not, generally, of the corpse, but 'from corpse': that is, a likeness taken from the features of the dead body would be used to paint a picture of an apparently living being. Sometimes the fact of death was acknowledged by the inclusion of discreet symbols of death; sometimes the family insisted that these be omitted. Such a portrait could be complete and hanging on the wall within a week of death.[5] Rarely (especially of course if a death occurred in an artist's family, although this does not apply in the following instance) a likeness would be produced by a member of the family:

> After the child was laid out, she looked so very beautiful that our mother took her pencil and sketched her likeness as she lay.[6]

With the introduction of photography, photographers, and champions of the new medium, went out of their way to promote it as an unprecedented means of preserving human likenesses beyond the grave:[7]

> No enchantress' wand could be more potent to bring back the loved ones we once cherished than could those faithful resemblances wrought out by this almost magic art of Daguerre. For true indeed has this art been termed magic, as it works with such unerring precision, and with such wonderful celerity, that it only requires the spells and incantations of the device to complete the task. . . . When the speaking eye and warm cheek of loved ones . . . shall have passed away and left only their impress upon the tablet, then, and not till then, will this art assert its true greatness.[8]

In 1854 the Webster Brothers of Louisville, Kentucky, declared it the 'legitimate business' of a daguerreotypist to:

> take the form and features of 'the loved ones at home', in such a way that when the eye rests on the 'shadow' of some departed friend it will become full of soul, which will cause the curtain of the past to 'roll back' and permit us to view our 'school boy days', when we gamboled on the green 'with light feet and lighter hearts'; this is the kind of photographs [sic] we should study to produce, and where before you is the reflection of a sage with nothing before or behind or around to attract the eye; then it is the *man* rises in all his former majesty before you, then it is that your *soul* sees the *man* himself, and until some heedless person calls you 'back to earth' you believe you are looking on a 'thing of life'. We do not like to see *premiums* awarded for fancy or *comic pictures*, it is not what the parent wants of the daughter, nor the wife of the husband, nor the brother of the sister, nor the lover of the beloved, but a true and faithful likeness.[9]

Samuel Morse appealed to the same desire for permanent images of loved ones, in advertising his studio in 1840:

> How cold must be the heart that does not love. How fickle the heart that wishes not to keep the memory of the loved ones for after-times. Such cold and fickle hearts we do not address. But all others are advised to procure miniatures at Professor Morse's Daguerreotype Establishment.[10]

How the studio photograph as a *commodity* might be transformed into a treasured memento was described by the editor of *Humphrey's Journal* in 1854:

> in our hands it is a mere article of commerce. But how changed when it is received by those for whom it was originally designed; they look upon every feature, and trace in the expression some happy remembrance. The care exhibited in the charge of this memento is marked by a gentleness known and prompted only by pure love or the warmest friendship. No price can rectify the loss. Such is the feeling in a case recently brought before us. On board of that ill-fated vessel, the San Francisco, was a Daguerreotype — it sunk with the vessel; its owner was saved, and with the warmest anxiety offered a reward of *five thousand dollars* for the recovery of that single impression. This fact is worthy of the consideration of those who are putting off obtaining Daguerreotype likenesses until a more convenient season.[11]

As might be the case with painted portraits, portrait photographs sometimes depicted people holding framed photographs of deceased loved ones. As with paintings, photographs were frequently taken immediately after death, especially of children, who were sometimes shown being nursed by their mother as if they still lived. If this seems morbid to us today, we should imagine, say, the parents of a dead child, who in their grief realize that they have no likeness of the child whom death has torn from them: now is their last chance to scrape together enough money to commission a portrait or pay for the services of a photographer. In our own time, photographs of deceased newborn babies, who have not lived long enough to be photographed alive, taken by parents or hospital staff, may be treasured by the parents and will help them to grieve (in contrast to misguided advice to forget all about it); drawings of ill and in some cases dying babies, made by the artist Heather Spears in a Danish hospital, were likewise greatly appreciated by the parents.[12]

The apparent 'magic' of photography in its early days on at least one occasion stimulated impossible demands:

> A lady and gentleman called in, and wished to be 'Daguerreotyped together'. When our arrangements were made, and they

were about to 'take a seat', the lady remarked, that she had lost a child about three months previous, and desired me to take them with her child upon her lap. As you may imagine, her husband was startled at her request.[13]

On another occasion an Irish man approached the photographer W. Campbell of Union City, New Jersey, asking for his wife who was 'dead and buried' to be photographed. Mr Campbell explained that a picture was not possible. The Irish man left after being assured that any material object could be pictured if put before the camera, rather than only the human face as he had supposed. Shortly after, he returned with a basket and

> proceeded to place the contents on the floor; first came a woman's bonnet, then a shawl, a gown came next, a pair of stockings and a pair of shoes emptied the basket, no; not quite, a small parcel carefully laid on one side was unrolled, and two oranges, one of them half sucked was laid beside the apparel. Amazed, we look on in silence; there was nothing there we could not take a picture of that was certain.

These preparations having been completed:

> 'Now then' said he, 'ye said ye could take a picture of anything I'd bring, them's the old woman's clothes; it's all I've left of her, an' if ye can give me a picture of them I'll be pleased'. At first we were at a loss to know if he were really serious, but there was no mistaking that when we looked in his face, so we proceeded to arrange the clothes in as artistic a fashion as our skill and the subject would permit. We took two pictures, both good, and after colouring them, with an extra touch to the orange at his own request, he took one, and we kept the other. 'Thankee Sir', said he, as he left, 'them's all I've got of the ould woman, they're sure to get scattered about, but when I looks at this, I shall think I see my wife. Thankee Sir'.[14]

This touching anecdote illustrates again how objects, and perhaps especially clothes, can be charged with identity, memories, and associations.

Gravestones, of course, are memorials to the dead, for which the surviving family choose appropriate words for a public statement of remembrance, and select from the range of head-stone, lettering, and embellishment offered by the monumental mason; the tending of the grave can be thought of within the broad context of family art, and the choice of flowers may be determined by the deceased persons' or family preferences. Gravestones sometimes have framed portrait photographs attached to them. 'Mourning pictures', embroidered or painted on silk in the first decades of the nineteenth century, functioned rather like tombstones in the house itself; sometimes made within the family, they might also be made for the family by young ladies such as Emmeline Grangerfields in *The Adventures of Huckleberry Finn*, and like tombstones they also employed a limited range of stock symbols (*including* tombstones, and weeping willows) and mottos. But in being given a place in the home they became part of it, part of the family's visual tradition, like those remarked on by Alta Gould Woolson in 1873, which had then been in place for several decades and concerning which she had this to say:

> . . . However faulty these objects might appear as works of art, they are beyond criticism as the products of beloved fingers, and are enshrined in a thousand sweet associations.[15]

Visitors to open-air museums in Denmark cannot help but notice how, on the walls of many a preserved farmhouse, can be seen a framed *minde* or memorial, comprising hand-written and decorated verses, sometimes embellished with rosettes of coloured paper, dedicated to the memory of someone who had died. The *minde* is thus an equivalent of the mourning picture and an antecedent of the portrait photograph, a clear instance of how someone could be recalled by means of something other than a pictorial likeness. (In some houses similar birthday greetings can also be seen, anticipating modern birthday cards and related to the continuing Danish practice of composing verses for birthdays, particularly 'round birthdays' which mark each decade of a lifetime.) Another way of remembering the dead was to employ locks of their hair, woven or braided into bracelets (for example), or contained in a tiny frame, or, similarly framed, made into a brooch (which sometimes also included a

Plate 8 *A traditional Danish 'minde'*, celebrating the life of a member of the family who died in 1871. (Den Fynske Landsby, Odense. Photograph: the author)

portrait photograph). Hair-work was a popular home craft in America during the second half of the nineteenth century, and of hair-work memorabilia the popular journal *Godey's Lady's Book* remarked:

Hair is at once the most delicate and lasting of our materials and survives like love. It is so light, so gentle, so escaping from the idea of death . . .[16]

Hair, which could be so 'escaping from the idea of death . . .'; clothes, so intimately personal to us, which we make part of our appearance; likenesses. These ingredients come together in one of the most splendid works of family art, a set of hooked rugs made by Mrs Eleanor Blackstone, of Lacon, Illinois, between 1880 and 1890. Hooked rugs, like quilts, were examples of 'femmage', of a process in which scraps of family history, in the form of worn-out clothes in particular, are recycled, incorporated into new artefacts for reasons of economy but also because in this way household objects are charged with family memories. As has been said of quilts:

. . . the quilters . . . worked out of piece bags containing scraps their mothers and grandmothers had placed there. The quilts were a compendium of family history, each person symbolized by a bit of textile.[17]

And as quilters bear witness:

. . . Different ones of my family are always appearing from one of those bags.[18]

It's so much fun to pick up these quilts and see everybody's dresses in it.[19]

Although the memories sewn into quilts were usually of this kind, encoded within the quilt's abstract mosaic, occasionally memories were visualized pictorially – as for example by Mrs Ina Grant of Vermont, who between 1939 and 1946 made a 'Memory Quilt' incorporating, among the usual scraps, 172 specially embroidered pieces of muslin, each illustrating a particular memory from her life and the life of her family.[20]

Hooked-rugs, like quilts, incorporated scraps of worn garments, for ever associated in the family's memory with the person whose garment it had been. The hooked rug as family art and as heirloom is wonderfully celebrated in this anonymous poem, called 'The Hooked Rug':

Plate 9 *Hooked Rug*, c.1885. Eleanor Blackstone, 94×117 in. (Collection: Greenfield Village and the Henry Ford Museum, Dearborn, Michigan)

I am the family wardrobe, best and worst
Of all generations, from the first:
Grandpa's Sunday-go-to-meetin' coat,
And the woollen muffler he wore at his throat;
Grandma's shawl, that came from Fayal;
Ma's wedding gown, three times turned and once let down,
Which once was plum but now turned brown;
Pa's red flannels, which made him itch;
Pants and shirts; petticoats and skirts;
From one or another, but I can't tell which,
Tread carefully, because you see, if you scuff me,
You scratch the bark of the family tree.[21]

Of six large rugs hooked by Eleanor Blackstone, four survive. All depict members of the family. One is designed around six vignettes, one each for each child including a daughter who had died in infancy and whose portrait is inscribed with the text 'Suffer little children to come unto me'. Each child is shown engaged in some characteristic pastime, with his or her favourite pet, as informally as in a snapshot; *actual strands of their hair* are woven into the individual portraits. Another Blackstone rug depicts a family picnic in the woods, and a third, showing the family congregated in front of their house on a snowy day, incorporates the words of Jesus (an apt text for this study of domestic variety), 'In my Father's house are many mansions'.[22]

In our world we create 'many mansions', worlds within the world, each one a world which is home and which, by virtue of the 'mirrors' and the memories, the furniture, textiles, family life, and thumbmarks woven into its fabric, reflects its inhabitants individually and *en famille*. Home is a world that is responsive.

7

Making the Most of the Best: The Family Album

Naturally we always want to look our best when being photographed for posterity. When going to a photographic studio to be photographed, families invariably dressed up, so that they appeared (in Mark Twain's words):

> too much combed, too much fixed up; and all of them uncomfortable in inflexible Sunday clothes . . .[1]

Itinerant photographers, though, could arrive unannounced: a picture of two children, taken by such a photographer outside their home in Salford without their mother's knowledge, was subsequently purchased by her but not without misgivings, for when she sent it to the children's elder brother who was away fighting in the First World War, she wrote this letter to accompany it:

> Dear Willie, do you know these two little children but do not take too much notice of how they are taken for they look a bit untidy but I did not know they were having their likeness taken but I thought I would bye [sic] one to let you have a look at there [sic] dear little faces for they are always talking about there [sic] Willie he will be pleased to see how big they have got. Bye bye love.[2]

Just as the formal painted portrait came to be complemented by relatively informal 'conversation pieces', so too 'studio' photographic portraits, and the formal group photographs, which then as now were produced by photographers who visited

Plate 10 *Jesse Thomas with his Five Children, c.1905.* Jesse, a widower, was about to take his children to the workhouse. They put on their best clothes, walked to the photographer's studio for this portrait, and then walked on to the workhouse. However, the workhouse refused to admit the children because their father was not unemployed, and the family managed to stay together: Robert, the youngest, went to school at the age of three to solve the problem of his father being unable to look after him during the day, and in later life he became a Lord Mayor of Manchester. (The Documentary Photography Archive, Manchester)

schools, were to be complemented by informal 'snapshots' taken by members of the family. Both types of photograph might appear in the family album; whereas for the one the subjects go out of their way to look their best, snapshots, or 'happy snaps', may be said to portray the family at its best in another sense, providing a record of holidays, special occasions, harmony, and good humour. Snapshots also tend to record the best of weather, if only because limitations of equipment and know-how have often meant waiting for the benefit of sunlight.

Plate 11 *Edward and May Bond pictured by an itinerant photographer outside their Salford Home.* When their mother sent the photograph to their elder brother Willie, who was away fighting in the First World War, she explained 'I did not know they were having their likeness taken but I thought I would bye one to let you have a look at there dear little faces . . .' (Documentary Photography Archive, Manchester)

Of course, when we know a picture is about to be taken, we invariably pose or smile towards the camera; if, for this reason, a snapshot depicts a forced or artificial grimace, or if in spite of a quest for spontaneity it is found guilty of freezing someone's features in an immobile expression distorted by stillness, its 'likeness' may be disputed, and certain photographs may be denied entry to – or at a later stage removed from – the family album. (If women tend to be particularly sensitive, that is hardly surprising in a society in which they are constantly obliged to compare their personal appearance with images of feminine beauty and glamour.)

Since the early days of popular photography, and encompassing the introduction of the movie camera too, home photography has had its own equivalent to the literature of 'homemaking' in the form of books, magazines, and magazine articles (the latter sometimes included in 'homemaking' publications) proffering advice on how to take 'better' photographs. (In the 'serious' literature on photography and film, family photography and home movie-making have of course hardly ever been mentioned, though this is changing now.) Insofar as the advice on offer has concerned technical matters or aesthetic qualities, many people have taken little or no notice: a comparison of home movies with 'How to do it' manuals indicates total disregard of advice to plan before shooting, a lack of interest in avoiding posing and self-consciousness, and a disinclination to be bothered with editing.[3] In home and family situations, the person behind the camera is another member of the family; he or she does not want to be caught up in any form of 'professionalism' or 'Art'; self-conscious responses to the camera acknowledge its presence (and that of the photographer), avoiding either an artificial, contrived appearance of spontaneity or the separation of the photographer from the group. Whereas it is sometimes nice to get shots of the family unobserved by them, it is hardly appropriate to habitually photograph them as if they were some kind of rare species of wild life to be studied from the concealment of a hide! However, although the givers of advice sometimes suggest a more wide-ranging approach – by suggesting, for example, that there could be

> dozens of dreary routines that you might someday be glad you filmed . . . Your route to work, your friends' houses, the same old tennis court, a plain old street bus . . .[4]

– there is a clear consensus, shared by home photographers

77

and writers on popular photography, that the ideal subjects for family photographs (taking into account the nature of the medium and − not least − the *cost* of film) are those special occasions which we strive to make, and to remember, as especially happy.

Family photographs, then, partly by accident, partly by intention, are mirrors which offer reassuring reflections. It has sometimes been suggested that in so doing they distort reality:

> Domestic snapshot photographs are comforting, emotive and stabilising − by capturing the best moments of our past they act as a reconstructor of our history, enabling us to remember the days which were good and remove from memory the ones which were bad.[5]

A not dissimilar criticism was levelled by Roland Barthes at the celebrated photographic exhibition, 'The Family of Man'. Tackling the way the exhibition, compiled from the work of professional and amateur photographers worldwide, focused on such universal themes as birth, childhood, love, and death, Barthes argued that the exhibition's portrayal of the human 'family' as reflected by lyrical photographs illustrating no more than truisms (everyone is born, dies, and so on), was mere sentimentality which ignored those crucial *differences* 'which we shall here quite simply call "injustices"'.[6] In other words, what matters is not that we all have birth in common, but that we are born in different, sometimes desperate, sometimes privileged, circumstances.

It is impossible not to agree with Barthes − although I believe he is guilty of underestimating the value of celebrating human togetherness, given that there are always those who carry the concept of *difference* to extremes − by, for instance, *denying* the humanity of a people or a race other than their own. 'The Family of Man' was an attempt to compile a global family album; it *did* employ the selectivity of the family album, concentrating on joyous or at least positive images; yet perhaps Barthes' strictures highlight an illuminating difference, that whereas 'The Family of Man', in choosing pictures of such a scattered family, inevitably removed images from their specific

78

contexts, the family album remains in the home, is compiled and contemplated by people who *do* remember more than the pictures themselves relate, and may be complemented too by personal diaries as well as by unrecorded memories.[7] Furthermore, family photographs can reveal, or fail to entirely conceal, more than was intended, as has been demonstrated by Robert U. Akeret in his book *Photoanalysis*[8] that derives from his use of family photographs in therapy. Snapshots, even formal photographs, and not least, sequences of photographs in albums, can betray tell-tale signs of more difficult or complex relationships than the family group suggests to a first glance or members of the family were willing to face up to at the time; in therapy, such photographs can help people to correct the distortions to which memory may be subjected, and to resolve buried problems; they may *also* provide positive images which can assist in the restoration of self-confidence. A striking example of the latter is an adult woman's response to a photograph of herself as a toddler:

'That's me', she said, somewhat disbelieving. . . . 'I'm going to have that photo enlarged, as big as life if possible, and I'm going to hang it conspicuously where I can't miss it, where it will follow me around my apartment. I want it in the open – to remind me of what I was, and can be again.'[9]

So it is not wholly correct to accuse family albums of *removing* from memory times which were bad. Family photography does not and indeed cannot erase anything; indeed, it cannot even determine with any certainty which memories will be triggered by its images, for a photograph can release a flood of memories from outside its own frame and moment. What family photography does do is to *choose* what it *particularly* wishes to remember; the photographer chooses a moment, an image, and the compilation of a family album involves choosing from among the resulting photographs and possibly choosing parts of photographs (which can be trimmed accordingly), constructing groups and sequences of images. Generally speaking, strife, illnesses, and anxieties are simply not photogenic so far as the family is concerned; they occur, but are dealt with, and are remembered, in other ways. Family photography combines spontaneity and design; given a loaded camera, 'snapping' a moment of joy or an expression of delight is a reflex action; the accumulation and organizing of photographs in family albums is a joyous, positive, creative, and possibly courageous strategy of making the most of happy times, constructing a mirror in which the family can see what it was, and can be again. It is in this light, I would suggest, that Val Williams' otherwise perceptive analysis of Vanessa Bell's family photography, 'using the snapshotter's familiar tools of bright light and happy occasions' to 'emphasise her belief in the success of her own construction of family life'[10] should be interpreted − not so much as an exercise in self-deception, more as a refusal to give up. There is nothing wrong or deceitful in using family photography constructively; there *may* be danger in one person (or even one generation) doing all the photography, unless he or she really is able to capture the family's authentic view of itself.

But to legitimize photographic practice of this kind, in this way, is not to define boundaries within which photography and the family album must always necessarily be confined. If family photography can be accused of salvaging uncharacteristically happy images from less than idyllic reality, it has also been used, startlingly and powerfully, to carry forward and to assert past times, in which those portrayed were alive and free and with their family, in a present from which they have been forcefully removed: in some countries, under oppressive regimes, women (in particular) have pointedly and publicly worn enlarged photographs of missing loved ones as placards hung from their necks. Consideration of such extreme and anguished circumstances may perhaps suggest that it is not necessary to idealize family life to appreciate it as a major component of 'normality'. The two case studies that will occupy us for the remainder of this chapter will demonstrate how sequences of photographs can go beyond 'happy snaps' in holding up a mirror to domestic life.

Jo Spence's exhibition 'Beyond the Family Album', described and illustrated in her 'political, personal and photographic autobiography',[11] arose out of her awareness of what is *not* depicted in family albums. This included, in the case of her mother, the 'sheer hard work involved in childcare', whereas 'Of my father's life as a worker I had no record at all'. As for herself:

> In my early photographs there is no record of my appalling health (or the many doctors who fobbed me off with under-developed medicines because of my unseen 'social problems'); no record of the pointless years shunted around schools inside formal education (where I was downgraded for 'unruly behaviour', constantly evaluated and eventually crushed into the mould of 'typist'); no record of a broken marriage and the havoc this so-called failure caused me; no record of hard work done for countless employers; no record of trying to please parents and other authority figures; no record of struggles. . . . Moreover, those 'happy', 'serious', 'loving', 'miserable' but always passive visual moments which do exist, those moments which only show surface information about me, give no indication at all of the wider social, economic and political histories of our disgusting class-divided society. They are rendered invisible within my 'family album'. (But then this is normal to most families, who are encouraged only to photograph their leisure, their consumption, or their ownership and to show the 'harmony' of their lives).[12]

This awareness, of 'gaping holes' in the photographic record of her life to date, led Jo Spence to scrutinize her current use of photography, and to reject photographic conventions and clichés — not least because as a professional photographer these had limited the ways in which she photographed other people besides herself — and to innovate. 'Beyond the Family Album' became part of the process of reassessment and change; in it she displayed a series of 'family' and 'private' photographs, of herself from infancy, with a commentary (including some penetrating 'photoanalysis'); a first photograph, of a naked baby of 8½ months, is juxtaposed with an equally naked woman, striking a similar pose, 'Five hundred and twenty eight months later'. In her own words, we see her deconstructing myself visually in an attempt to identify the process by which I had been 'put together'.[13]

That is, without actually disowning these images of herself as a child and young adult, she looks behind them, to see what they did not show, juxtaposes them with her buried memories, and in so doing learns how an unequal struggle to establish her own identity (complicated and hindered not so much by family difficulties as by wider issues of gender and class) led her to adopt poses, reflected by the camera's 'mirror with a memory', which are tentative tryings-on of ready-made stereotypes. If her family can be said to have let her down, it was not through negligence or lack of love but rather, as a result of being them- selves the victims of external pressures; theirs was the failure of 'homemaking', of submitting too much to society's expectation and imposition to nourish the growth and creating of authentic identity. (At the same time it is clear from Jo Spence's narrative that assessment of her upbringing must take full account of the traumatic effects of the Second World War, and particularly of evacuation, as a result of which 'we felt the adults had aban- doned us'.) In her late adolescence, desperate to leave home but forbidden to do so, Jo Spence recalls 'We had a family group taken of our 'happy days' together . . .' – a perhaps equally desperate attempt by her parents, surely not to tell a deliberate lie, but to seek a confirming reflection of what they had sought to construct before it was too late.

These photos from the past are followed by newer photo- graphs in which Jo Spence explores various images of herself, showing how, for example, contemporary depictions of women in advertising can influence the way in which people see them- selves or wish to be or are seen by others (e.g. 'Mark II tart. This picture is not about my sexuality, but is about my visually bantering with a particular stereotype'). 'Beyond the Family Album' is a brave, pioneering reclaiming of the right to be oneself, and to create images that mirror oneself as one really is – and in Jo Spence's case, to come to terms with 'a face and body you don't really like'. It prepares the ground for her to cope with, and to record photographically, the devastating experience of cancer of the breast. And it *is* a matter of going 'beyond' the family album rather than opposing it; the family album is incorporated and enlarged; the creativity inherent in family art is seized, through an amalgam of text and photography, to shape a life of one's own. Nor is Jo Spence above including, at the end of her sequence, a group of pictures 'for no better reason than they remind me of happy times and of people I love'.

If I hesitate to claim 'Beyond the Family Album', a work of radical and determined individuality, as a work of *family* art, I feel no such hesitation in the case of *Gramp*, a sequence of photographs with accompanying text published in 1976,[14] a remarkable example of family art through which a family has pushed out the boundaries of family photography and the family album.

Gramp is a photographic record, enhanced by a text that includes 'snapshots' of speech captured by the tape-recorder and extracts from personal journals, of one man's 'involvement' with senility, culminating in his death. The man was Frank Tugend; the photographs were taken by his grandsons, Mark (a professional photographer) and Dan Jury, in the course of their involvement in the family's caring of him; Mark was responsible for compiling the text.

The nature of the book as a family album is made clear by the first section, called 'Family Album', which uses family photographs to briefly relate the story of Frank Tugend's life from his birth, in Scranton, Pennsylvania, until he began to fail in July 1970. The first photograph is a studio portrait taken about 1900. Frank started work in the local mines, as a slate picker, at the age of eleven; his obituary in *The Scranton Tribune*, reprinted in the book, records that he retired 'after 54 years as hoisting engineer for the Glen Alden and Moffat Coal Cos'. His marriage in 1917 is recorded by another studio portrait, showing husband and wife against a painted arboreal background. A snapshot of 1918 portrays 'Frank, Anna and Baby Anna' who was to be Mark and Dan's mother. In 1924 the family is seen complete, Anna having been joined by a sister, Florence (or 'Nink', who was to remain at home with her parents and become one of the family team responsible for caring for Frank in his last years), and a son, named after his father, whose death in a plane crash in 1944 broke his father's heart — the 'one event' to mar a 'happy life in the country'. For in 1924 Frank purchased some land in the woods and, moving the family into a 'hastily constructed garage . . . began excavating for a house'. The family moved in when the basement was complete; Frank continued building the house literally over their heads.

Some later family photographs were taken by Mrs Tugend, and Mark's text recalls how much *his* family, resident in Indiana, loved spending 2 weeks each summer with the Tugends, 'At Christmastime we were still savoring the memories of the glorious days in July.' Several photos, taken between 1947 and 1957, show Mark and Dan with their grandfather, happy in each other's company.

The photographs of Frank Tugend's last years, the bulk of this 'album', are not entirely different in kind from the other family photographs. Asked 'When did you decide to photograph Gramp?', Mark replies:

> We never did 'decide' to take pictures, since we have always photographed our family. At both houses, a camera is usually within reach, and often either Dan or I will squeeze off a few shots. We photographed before Gramp became senile and we continue to photograph our lives.[15]

The last three photographs in the book comprise, first, a photo of Frank lying in state in an open coffin, surrounded by flowers — an image which perhaps sounds morbid, but which is made positively joyous by the additional presence of a very young great grandchild crawling on the floor in the foreground; second, by a happy family group photographed to celebrate the fifth birthday of an older grandchild, Hillary; and thirdly, by another picture involving Hillary, which I will describe below.

But *why* did Mark and Dan photograph Frank's decline so closely (for it is an intimate, daily record; a photographic journal)? And why did they seek or agree to the *publication* of the resulting 'album'? These questions are not posed; a tentative answer to the first question is given and, though not complete, is illuminating:

> We really began photographing Gramp's condition, however, when he required 'babysitting'. Whenever Dan or I watched him, we photographed him as a way to pass the time. Gramp never minded the camera and long after he had forgotten who we were he recognized that the person with the camera was a friend, and he would stay close to whoever had the camera.[16]

Because of the family's longstanding use of photography, then, the camera, far from presenting a threat to a confused old man, provided a last link of failing recognition between him and his family. Further clues as to why the photographs were made are apparent in the photographs themselves, which demonstrate just how much family life revolved around caring for 'Gramp' right up until the last day when 4-year-old Hillary sits with him:

> I'm in my slimy worm suit, and he liked me to hold his hand. I thought he was pretty nice and lovable. This is the last day. He died that night.[17]

The family's tradition of photography could not have been continued without including Frank as a central figure; these years of caring constituted a major family project, something they undertook *together*. As to why the visual record was published, I believe answers can be detected in references to local people disapproving of the family taking Frank to local events in his 'condition'; in mention of how former regular visitors ceased to call; and in the family's courageous and surely right decision to care for Frank at home, to let him die in the house he built with his own hands, in spite of the option of sending him to a nursing home:

> We . . . learned that Gramp would undoubtedly be 'subdued' (strapped down) should he go to a nursing home — since the institution wouldn't tolerate his wandering ways.[18]
>
> . . . We also had to decide in the last weeks whether or not to have him hospitalized to be sustained by intravenous tubes. But after he had made it clear that he *wanted* to die, we chose to let him die at home, with some dignity intact.[19]

Paradoxically, though perhaps not everyone would agree, these pictures of a man at his least dignified do confer on him − or perhaps more accurately, recognise *in* him − a kind of dignity *in spite of*; they do so through *attending*, as distinct from ignoring and keeping out of sight; overall, the book portrays an individual's struggle against the odds, and his final choice to let go is movingly conveyed. The book, then, is a family album become a public statement, not of how families must behave, but of how they may choose to cope; like (though unlike) Carl Larsson's books, it provides encouragement, and inspires confidence, by *example*.

Gramp demonstrates that there is no need to eliminate difficulties and stress from the family record, particularly where these are coped with in a context of love and solidarity. They can be safely remembered, in the knowledge that happier times will shine through:

> Of one thing I am sure. No matter how many times I have to clean Gramp, or feed him, or blow his nose, or care for him in the middle of the night when my body only wants to ignore him, I will always remember the good times with Gramp before I recall the bad.[20]

Even difficulties can be transfigured, by love and by humour, for instance, so that at least some 'good' can be discerned in them. In this case members of the family

> learned a lot about Gramp, and about one another. All of us, though, learned even more about themselves.

In adversity people discover what they are but didn't know they were capable of, individually and together. It is a learning experience for children, too, and not without some fun. '. . . We would miss the craziness he brought into our lives'.[21]

Finally, to return to the very last photograph, which shows a splendid mobile of fish shapes in the children's room, with Frank's great grandchildren painting at a table in the background. In his senility, Frank had imagined creatures and characters which he had given names to − chillysmiths, bugeyes — whose reality only Hillary had been able to share, and which she remembered after his death:

> 'Why do you remember those imaginary characters so vividly?'
> I asked her one day.
> 'They're not imaginary', she retorted with conviction, 'they're real. They're not pretend'.
> 'They moved over to our house', she confided to me in conspiratorial tones, 'they tied strings together and made themselves into a mobile in my room. They look like fish now. They remind me of Gramp'.[22]

Thus the (home-made?) mobile is, or has taken on properties of, family art, charged with memories, a link between the living and the dead, and for Hillary a token of her special involvement in an experience which gave her an early and valuable acceptance of ageing and death.

8

Marking Time:
Ritual and Ceremony

Art is a form-giving activity, a making of marks, objects, constructions. Family art not only helps us to make, and put our mark upon, a home in three dimensions; it can also help us to structure our dwelling in *Time*; to mark time; to shape our lives from beginning to end.

Even at its most mundane and everyday, our living can benefit from organization, not simply for the sake of utility but also because, through our deliberate shaping of it, passing time becomes another mirror in which we can see ourselves reflected as purposive and creative, capable of taking control of it rather than letting it roll over us. For a family, designing and operating a daily routine is likely to be essential from a purely practical point of view, but it also reflects something of that family's corporate identity and perhaps, its capacity for working together through consensus and mutuality; indeed, family rituals often *become* ritualized precisely because members of the family want a particular practice to be repeated, and then to be repeated *ad infinitum* because the more it is repeated the more it feels 'right'; very probably it will include features inherited from previous generations. And it may well incorporate, and safeguard, special times when a family make a point of being together and of celebrating their togetherness.[1]

As with other aspects of homemaking and family life, the temporal ordering of daily life necessarily involves responding to the outside world as well as innovating within the home; to a degree, the routines of different families may be variations on a theme. Jeremy Seabrook has vividly and sensitively evoked how it was that, for generations of British working class people, 'the weekdays were not the same; each was associated with a different consciousness that stained them all a different colour'.[2] The week began with a 'reluctant sense of renewal' on Monday mornings; it continued through a quickening of life in mid-week, found its best moment in the happy relaxation of Friday evening, and closed with the quietness of Sunday and the melancholy of Sunday evening ('the time of the week when people got closest to each other: unity in the face of the time when the ritual would finally finish; a contemplation of mortality, afterlife'). Events which punctuated the shifting quality of the days included the washing of clothes and linen on Monday; cleaning the house on Friday; football on Saturday afternoon; a long lie-in, Sunday dinner, and relatives visiting for tea on Sundays. This structuring of the week served and was largely dictated by utility; as Seabrook remarks, 'Time was so densely structured that it seemed closed to all innovation and change.' Yet structuring had its positive side, making time almost as physical, as visible, and as reassuring as the house itself: indeed, like the house, it became an inhabited construction that gave shelter, was 'cradling and comforting' and dependable. When I went away to boarding school at the age of eleven, it was important to me to be able to recall the daily round at home and depend on its continuing, so that, at such and such a time, I could think to myself 'Now they will be sitting down to lunch', or morning coffee or bedtime cocoa or whatever.

The pressures of the daily round might seem to offer little scope for innovation, but the creativity of families, and not least of women (in spite of intense burdens and powerful stereotyping) cannot be written off; indeed, it only needs a certain way of *seeing* to transform the humblest domestic task into ceremony, a rite of blessing the house, of thanksgiving. Lines by the poet Gillian Clarke are worth quoting a second time:

> It is easy to make of love
> these ceremonials. As priests
> we fold cloth, break bread, share wine . . .[3]

Given the spirit of family art, it becomes easy to make – to *re*create – the daily round unique to each family, however much its bare bones may be dictated by necessity; to adapt it to be hospitable to the needs and personalities of members of the family; to incorporate elements that are consciously designed to be just so, to be relatively formal, say, to mark the time, the moment, the occasion. Family prayers once marked the beginning of the day in many a household; a grace or (in a Quaker or agnostic family) a few moments' silence may still precede a meal. Children's bedtime and the end of their day are also likely to be more or less structured, maybe including reading a book aloud, telling a story, a review of the day's events, a lullaby, a prayer. Cooking is an art: the preparation and presentation even of everyday meals can include an element of deliberate 'art', or may incorporate such impromptu inventiveness as this, recalled long after from the winter breakfasts of childhood:

> My mother . . . made treacle animals and birds on my slices of bread. She'd dip the spoon into the dark treacle and twirl it around, then we'd wait as it came down with a quick plop onto the bread magically forming itself into a bird, a pig or a rabbit. It wasn't hunger that made me eat three or four slices: it was that I couldn't bear not to see another shiny creature appear on yet another piece of bread.[4]

The creation of mealtimes is beautifully evoked by Lucy Boston in one of the volumes of her 'Green Knowe' series of children's books. Ping, a refugee, is staying with Mrs Oldknow (who lives in Lucy Boston's own, real, house and surely shares much of Lucy Boston's own character?):

> Ping loved the meals he had with Mrs Oldknow. There was just enough ceremony to make each occasion feel like a special one. It was not discipline that cramped but a ceremony that one could play with and expand and even laugh at. *It made him feel really at home.*[5] [My italics]

The point is not overworked, but clearly Ping appreciates this element of order and formality all the more for having been homeless, a refugee from chaos and disorder, and this illuminates the value of rite and ceremony in offering security and certainty to all of us, children not least. Domestic ceremony *is* home, and it embodies love.

Meals link the everyday with special occasions, in the ceremonials of which they so often feature; it is also noteworthy that meals and special occasions can link the world of home with the world outside. Meals (for the fortunate) measure our days; Sunday lunch rounds off the week; occasions mark both the seasons of the year, and the unfolding of family life and of individual lives within the family: anniversaries of several kinds, and annual occurrences and festivals, mark out our lives together. Sometimes we may mark time very literally, counting the days to an eagerly anticipated occasion, for instance, as when we open the numbered doors of Advent calendars (carefully chosen if not home-made) on the days preceding Christmas. A number of years ago I used this same principle to make a calendar for our young son, so that he could open a window and find a surprise picture every day while I was away on a lengthy trip abroad: each opened window brought our reunion nearer. (Apart from Advent calendars, I may also have been inspired by memories of the 'end-of-term' charts we used to make at boarding school, as a means of counting down the days until the holidays). Birthdays, including comings-of-age, and events such as christenings and first communions are occasions for the family to pay special attention to one of its members; the identity of that individual is mirrored and celebrated by the occasion; another stage in his or her life is marked out. Family names and dates, at least of birth and death, may be recorded on the flyleaf of a family Bible. In parts of Europe, and in Pennsylvanian German communities in the United States, birth and baptisms, and more rarely, marriages, were marked by the production of elaborate, calligraphic documents, often the work of the local teacher: these recorded the date and time of birth and the parents' names, were treasured by their owners all their lives, were very often kept in the family Bible or were pasted inside the lid of a Bible box or linen chest, and at death were sometimes placed in the coffin, as if as a passport to the next life. Sometimes the date of marriage or of death was

Plate 12 *A Calendar of an Absence,* made by the author for his young son using the principle of the Advent Calendar.

pencilled onto the bottom or the reverse of a *fraktur* (as they were called). In Germany, it is still customary for parents to present a child with a brightly decorated cardboard cornucopia full of sweets, when he or she goes to school for the first time. Mothering Sunday in Britain (the fourth Sunday in Lent) and Mother's Day in the United States (the second Sunday in May) provide, in addition to her birthday, an opportunity for children to make a fuss of 'the best mother in the world, your mother'. Although these two separate occasions have been confused, and are nowadays promoted by commerce as well as by churches, Sunday and day schools, the element of family art in the bunch of violets or home-made greetings card is not to be denied. Neither can such a celebration be ruled altogether inappropriate so long as women bear the brunt of domesticity, though it clearly represents a culmination and confirmation of the defining of woman's role and the stereotyping noted earlier in this book.[6]

Portrait likenesses, and things with which they were identified, recall the dead; *ritual* can help families to cope with death when it happens: it provides a means of marking the end of a life at the time it occurs, and of inaugurating a new series of anniversaries. Thereafter, that time each year, though allowed to pass quietly, will be kept as a time of special remembering in the hearts and minds of those close to the deceased. Family art can help the family to mourn, to give expression to its grief, and (as we have seen) to remember. The arts of mourning comprise both the making of memorials, *and* rite and ceremony: the wake, the funeral, the observing of a period and of the forms of mourning. All of these are activities of making *signs*, of marking an end: the funeral ceremony is a visible sign for its duration; it may also be the occasion for the distribution of permanent tokens (such as inscribed mourning spoons) to the gathered mourners. Swedish *majning*, the laying down of branches in front of the house of the deceased, is the making of a temporary sign, as is the wearing of mourning dress. The tombstone, a permanent, public, sign, is likely to become the scene and object of private ceremonies of the tending of the grave.

Except in 'Modern' times and societies, families have not

been encouraged to withdraw entirely into solitary, private mourning. The wake was an occasion for the whole community; *majning* was the marking of a death by means of a public sign. The quilting community, always ready to turn out quilts for those in particular need, characteristically did what they could at the time of a death:

> When I was about four years old the neighbour's baby died . . . the men was [sic] making the casket . . . [the women] quilted the lining for the casket, and then they made a tiny little quilt out of blue silk to cover the baby.[7]

In its grief the bereaved family would find itself drawing strength from a larger family which drew together to heal the wound in its fabric. The community expected grief to be expressed publicly and properly; no doubt family pride helped it to meet the expectation that it should bear its grief openly but with dignity: thus that very expectation could be helpful and supportive. The rites of grieving at once provided distraction from the grief itself (the blessing, in such circumstances, of having something to do) and channelled it into a means and form of expression.

In our time we have put aside traditional arts of mourning, as if hoping, by paying it less attention, that death will go away. When it does catch up with us, we are ill-equipped to cope with it. Just as the twentieth century has largely deprived us of the right to be born at home, so too we have allowed it to discourage us from dying at home, and after death our bodies are tidied away and disposed of, swiftly, hygienically, 'aesthetically'. Rather than relieving the family of its burden of grief, this undermines and cuts away opportunities for expressing grief, while neighbours may remain blissfully unaware that a death has occurred. And, as with the furnishing and decorating of our homes and the making of greetings cards and personal gifts, we have allowed commerce to move in and do for us, at a price, what we ought to do ourselves (at one time the family laid out its own dead: the community knew better than to usurp the family's place though it might provide women to assist). Thus death has been turned into a business, with its own range of clichés for sale; in this as any market, differences are confined to how much can be afforded. The modern funeral is a lonely and empty gesture in an impersonal language.

It need not be so. In a volume published in 1965, Geoffrey Gorer drew attention to the 'potentially important roles played by ritual', and by society, in 'giving help to the mourner . . . and assisting him in giving expression to and working through his distress'. This aspect of mourning, said Gorer, had at that time 'barely been touched on by previous writers'.[8] More recently, Nils-Arvid Bringeus concluded an essay on the arts of mourning with a moving appeal, made on behalf of the community:

> When symbols are impoverished and rituals are altered to a conventional minimum, the work of mourning is made more difficult. Don't make death a private matter, but give us back our possibility of participating and helping.[9]

To cope with death, we need family art that is private and personal but can also open into the arts and rites of the 'family' of a supportive community.

In addition to helping the family to mark out and to celebrate the lives of its members, family art, allied to and enhancing ritual, contributes to the structuring of the year, grounding us in the rhythm of the seasons, that primordial calendar into which human beings have variously fitted their calendars of work and school and holiday, of play and games and sport, and not least, of their spiritual life (Christmas in the northern hemisphere being forever identified with mid-winter, and Easter with spring). High days and holidays are very much family occasions and often the occasion for family reunions; family art will rise to the occasion and make it more memorable. That this can happen in the absence of wealth or training or privilege of any kind, and despite the 'density' of lives of struggle from which opportunity had been largely forced out, is illustrated by Robert Roberts' recollection of his family's annual New Year's Eve celebrations in the slums of Salford. This was a theatrical event in which his father acted as compere and to which every member of the family contributed from a stage of soapboxes, 'Ellie always reciting 'Ring out, wild bells, to the wild sky' as a finale'. And then came a solemn ritual; their father would go outside 'whatever the weather', and the family left within listened to the silence just before midnight until it was broken by an

> indescribable clamour; as midnight struck and factories, docks, ships and shunting engines whistled and hooted. Now Father pounded on the door, Mother opened it, and from the light of the street lamp across we saw them embrace, softly, my father folding her to him. 'A happy New Year!' . . . Only once in a year they 'loved' each other like this. Then, gaily, both came . . . to kiss and hug us in our turn. Back in the kitchen, every gas mantle glowing, we sang

> Hail, smiling morn . . .[10]

Christmas is the festival of home and family *par excellence*. To acknowledge this is not to detract from its central significance; its celebration of a birth and its contemplation and re-enactment of giving, as well as its pagan ancestry as a mid-winter making and celebrating of rare comfort, of warmth and light, and of conviviality, complement and enhance one another:

> The central figure of the child, God coming to Earth, the giving of gifts, the element of peace and warmth in the middle of winter – this modern cult of Christmas responded to some of the deepest aspirations of the bourgeois spirit.[11]

For John Lukacs, the author of these words, whose championing of what he calls the 'bourgeois spirit' involves defining it in much the same terms as I will define and champion the values implicit in family art, our 'modern' family Christmas is perfectly reflected in the carol 'Silent Night' with its 'sense of a sublime equilibrium, a sublime stillness'. At Christmas family art comes into its own; the home is transformed, by decorations, the tree, a crib; greetings cards, which like decorations and the crib may be home-made, are sent out, received, displayed; presents are made, or chosen, and are carefully, lovingly, wrapped and labelled, and exchanged in ceremonies of giving; meals are

Plate 13 'Christmas Preparations': an illustration from a magazine of c.1880 by J. G. Franz.

created, with considerable art, and are ceremonially shared. And the re-creation of the interior of the home is given outward sign, in lit Christmas trees placed in windows, garlands on front doors. In short, the potential for family creativity, in the space of these precious few days of each year, is tremendous. At Christmas, we share a public festival, which each family interprets in its own way.

Christmas will shed its special light on other parts of this book; in *this* context a single example will suffice to illustrate how family ritual begins, is sustained, evolves, and functions. In one American family, when the daughter was 3 years old, her father held her on his lap on Christmas Eve and read to her Clement Moore's verses 'A Visit from St Nicholas'. Every Christmas Eve after that, the reading was repeated; the audience was enlarged by the birth of another daughter, and the ceremonial nature of the event developed. As the two girls grew older, they sat on either side of their father on the sofa; mother and other relatives joined the company; refreshments were served after the reading, and the conversation turned around recollections of earlier Christmases. Further elaborations – emphasizing the visual aspect of the ceremony – included turning off the lights and lighting candles. As the girls grew up, nothing could keep them from being at home on Christmas Eve. After their respective marriages, both girls returned to their parents' home with their husbands, and then with husbands and children, each Christmas Eve, to be present at the ceremony.[12]

This ceremony – which will have equivalents in the experience of many families – began with spontaneous innovation, a father's responding to Christmas (and perhaps his own memories) on the one hand, and to his young daughter on the other; it was repeated by popular demand, gradually becoming more and more embedded in the family's Christmas until no one could imagine doing without it; it served to mark one particular day each year; by celebrating Christmas Eve together in this way the family implicitly but insistently celebrated and reinforced their own togetherness, and in a way which eventually reached into and embraced new families and three generations.

9

A Child's World

Children are involved in family art both as subject matter and as participants. They feature prominently in family portraits and photographs, and indeed it is often the desire to record the passing events and images of childhood, which more than anything else, stimulates family photography. The once common ache to remember children who died in infancy is paralleled by a comparable wish to remember children as they were, at the different ages and stages, which for parents can seem to pass (or to *have* passed) all too quickly. But family art, in making home the family's own world, does more than merely depict children for the sake of their parents; it nourishes and accommodates them as active inhabitants of that world, contributors of thumbmarks to its doors, beings who recognize themselves as readily in thumbmarks as photographs, *most* readily in their own creativity and clutter with which many a family home is likely to be engulfed. In its homemaking activities, family art sets out to make of the home a world in which children in particular will feel at home; in which they will discover who they are and that they belong; through their experience of which they will learn that 'world' is partly something given, to which one has to adjust, and partly something one can recreate or create in (and thereby *extend*); and *from* which they will by degrees, and finally, confidently, venture forth.

Home, then, is a staging post, family life a rite of passage, between womb and world. Home exists to enable us, from childhood, to feel 'at home' in the universe. And home is four dimensional; it exists in Space *and* Time. Enveloped within the womb, the unborn child experiences the sound of its mother's heartbeat as a first measure of Time, rhythmic, reliable; as adults we sometimes feel threatened by the passing of time, but that we find the regular ticking of a clock reassuring is surely due to an inner awareness that if Time ceased, so would we, and also to the fact that it makes Time *real*? Young children need to feel secure within, and convinced of the reality of, a sheltering world, a world which exists in Space and Time, the reality of which is our reality. The natural structures of Time — night and day, the seasons — are accommodated and enhanced within the home; home is preparation for and interacts with the physical, social, and temporal structures of the wider world: the calendar and daily timetable of school, for instance. The importance of Time in children's lives is demonstrated by the fact that they become its chief priests and priestesses: '. . . juvenile activities are the most *living* calendar celebrations in Britain, for they are the most spontaneous'.[1] At Christmas the resources of family art are deployed both to decorate, enrich, and reaffirm the *house*, and also to mark a yearly cycle, for Christmas is for many children the most eagerly anticipated time of the whole year and it brings with it — or rather, we bring to it — its own season of longing and preparation, its own strict schedules of celebration.

Home, for a child, is a world within the world: a compact, companionable world, brimful of love and happiness; a world that provides a base for sorties and exploration beyond its safe territory; a first grounding in reality. As such it is a world which we carry with us for ever:

> . . . The house we were born in is physically inscribed in us. It is a group of organic habits. After twenty years, in spite of all the other anonymous stairways, we would recapture the reflexes of the 'first stairway', we would not stumble on that rather high step. The house's entire being would open up, faithful to our being. We would push the door that creaks with the same gesture, we would find our way in the dark to the distant attic. The feel of the tiniest latch has remained in our hands.[2]

Although even home cannot be eternally invulnerable to

change, if we are lucky its relative constancy (and at least its constancy in our remembering of it) serves a purpose, anchoring our growing-up. No doubt because we never lived in a house that we could regard either as a permanent home or as truly our own, the continuity of the timetable of our family life, which could be reasserted in every house we moved to, was particularly important to me – and remained so, to a degree, into adult life; when my father finally retired and my parents were able to buy a small house of their own, that long established way of life (which had of course imperceptibly evolved) was at last allowed to settle into place. Peter Townsend, condensing the essence of several conversations with old people, has revealed that the old may want to stay put in their own homes not simply for their own sake or because they like to be surrounded by the stuff of their lives, but also for the sake of their grown-up children who like to be able to revisit the home they grew up in, perhaps to share it a little with their own children:

> Home was the old armchair by the hearth, the creaky bedstead, the polished lino with its faded pattern, the sideboard with its picture gallery and the lavatory with its broken latch. . . . It embodied a thousand memories and held promise of a thousand contentments. It was an extension of personality. To the married children it was also the reminder of their history and achievements – this the chair scorched by a sparkler on Guy Fawkes night, this the wallpaper where you looked for animal shapes, that the doormat that had to be lifted at the corner if the door was to be shut. 'We always go over *home* to see Mum on Sundays', said a married daughter. Part of what the children felt for their parents was what they felt for the parental home. It was not only the place where associations with the past and long usage provided comfort and security in old age. It was a symbol of family unity and tradition.[3]

John Burnett, commenting on some unpublished autobiographical texts dating from the 1820s to the 1920s, noticed how frequently and how vividly adults recall the 'material culture', so to speak, of childhood – the house, furniture, objects;[4] Wordsworth's

101

old familiar doors,
Hearths loved in childhood, and ancestral floors.[5]

This was no less true, perhaps more so, of many poor homes, where the few possessions were endowed with peculiar significance, one or two simple toys might be played with again and again until worn beyond all repair, and senses uncluttered by excess received the impact of what there was with all the richness it had to offer – the grain of wood, pattern of curtain and wallpaper, texture and colours of a hooked rug. A negative side to all this is represented by the pain that children can suffer as a result of having to leave a beloved house or even of being parted from a particular object: Sabra Moore, a contemporary artist, has used her art to recall a home-made bed over which, discarded during her childhood, she kept vigil during its final hours.[6]

The world of childhood, remembered in adult life, shows us how to create a comparable world for *our* children. In one of her stories for children in which she draws heavily on her own fund of memories, the Swedish author Astrid Lindgren tells of a birthday of birthdays when a 7-year-old, who has hitherto shared a room with her brothers, is blindfolded by her parents, turned around and around, and led into another room where the blindfold is removed:

> It all looked so lovely that I almost thought a wizard must have been in there. Mother said, yes, there had been a wizard around and that the wizard was Father, and that he had conjured up a room for me that was to be my very own. This was my birthday present, she said.

Her father had wallpapered the room and had himself made 'a whole chest of drawers, *and* a round table, *and* a shelf, *and* three chairs' which he had also painted. Her mother had made the curtains and also 'the rag mats that lay on the floor and which had red, yellow and green edges'.[7]

A world – her own room – in a world – home – in a world. But of course, parents know not to do everything for their children,

Plate 14 *A child's drawing of her family*. Polly Baynes included dead as well as living members of the family in this drawing of her family riding on a train. (Ken and Kate Baynes)

and not, always, to impose their own taste, but to tolerate and indeed positively encourage children's own creativity, to let them express themselves (including their feelings about the family, love, anger, grief at a bereavement), to let them make *their* mark on the home. Children's paintings and drawings should have their place in the family's visual tradition and everyday surroundings; children should have some say in the decoration and arrangement of their own space. For Astrid Lindgren's young heroine, the sheer magic of delighted surprise more than adequately substituted for the satisfaction she might have experienced had she been involved in planning her room; and of course, the room was only begun, and remained to be inhabited.

Of course, children have their own perspective on the home they share with their parents. They see it closer to; it does not yield to them many of the memories which it holds for their parents; they identify with their 'own' objects and spaces, with what they make and with what they leave behind in their wake; they have a capacity to burrow further in and — by their own routes — out. For them the world of home can contain smaller, more intimate, worlds.

To be satisfactory a world has to be, safe and secure, certainly, but not totally shut-in on itself. It has to be have doors and windows, openings, views, ways out into excitement and danger. Openings into other worlds, whether actual or imaginary, to be explored, escaped into, inhabited, are essential to childhood, and family art can help to provide them.

The least that is required is somewhere to be quiet, private, hidden; somewhere where day-dreams can be released to float for a while undisturbed like soap bubbles; perhaps somewhere that understanding parents set aside for a child or which a child claims for its own. It is to our shame that we have mastered the miserable art of building houses *without* nooks and crannies, attics or cellars or interesting spaces, and that we have reduced gardens to pocket-handkerchief-sized areas devoid of excitement or concealment and exposed in all their poverty to a single glance; yet a comfortable, accommodating armchair or the garden swing may suffice. Through story-telling, or in the shared enjoyment of books and of radio or television, the whole family can enter another realm; beloved characters from that kingdom may be brought back to share home with the family, featuring in its conversation, for instance, embodied in a soft toy, perhaps, or like Father Christmas entering through the agency of faith but performing a very real task and leaving tangible evidence (mincepie crumbs, a drained brandy glass). All of this is part and parcel with family art in the broadest sense. But also, worlds within the world of home can be actually visible, brought into being by hand and craft (or purchase) as well as by imagining.

The making of worlds within the home can range from the temporary transformation of a room and its furniture into a Red

Indian camp or a pirate ship, to the sturdily built play house in the garden advocated by Gertrude Jekyll[8] — a roomy affair fully-equipped for tea-parties, and with a garden all its own! Or it can vary from spontaneous, ephemeral ad-hocism to the skilled modelling of a miniature world in perfect detail. Robert Roberts tells how as a child his two older sisters once built for him

> a splendid Greek temple from half-pound blocks of Sunlight soap . . . and carton board, with rows of candles for columns — all based on a picture in *Harmsworth's Self-Educator*. Inside they put a night light on a low altar — the 'eternal flame' which, according to our reading, no decent temple could be without. Then Mother, turning out the gas to 'get the full effect', came to admire. 'Really Greek!' she said. It took her back three thousand years! This delighted us, because she didn't praise overmuch.[9]

Improvisation of exactly this kind was advocated by Edith Nesbit, celebrated author of *The railway children*, who in a remarkable but sadly neglected book, *Wings and the child* (1913) founded a complete, and a wise, philosophy of parenthood and education almost entirely on her enthusiasm for building whole cities from bricks and bits and pieces around the house. Her own efforts are splendidly illustrated and much practical advice is proffered.[10] Altogether more sophisticated, as well as relatively permanent, are such things as model railway layouts, with perfectly scaled buildings and scenery, inhabited by tiny figures (and, through the imagination, by onlooker and participant regardless of age), while in this author's personal opinion nothing can equal a model railway in the garden. As a child I was enchanted by some pictures in a book that my father had kept from his boyhood, in which a model railway, with a train actually driven by steam, a model water-mill with a water-wheel turned by a stream tumbling into a lake, and a 'windmill' in the form of a wooden figure with revolving arms, all in one large garden, were used by the garden's owner and creator, a Mr Blake, to demonstrate to a visiting small boy (and to the slightly less fortunate reader) the power of wind, water, and steam.[11] I have never forgotten the fascination of those pictures nor their demonstration of how a garden can be made into a

Plate 15 *Elephant Temple*, a construction made by E. Nesbit to demonstrate how buildings and cities can be created from household objects. From her book *Wings and the Child* (1913).

whole world, and I was reminded of them when I built a much less sophisticated garden railway for our sons (and, at long last, for myself). Model farms for children to play with can also be quite elaborate indoor affairs or can be improvised on carpet, bedspread, or, best of all, in the garden on sunny summer days. Robert Roberts did not have a farm, but one day when he was alone with his mother she hit on the idea of making hay; together they gathered grass from a nearby brickfield, spread it

out in the sun on the low scullery roof, turned it the next afternoon, and then

> At last we made what she called a 'haycock' and sat it on the
> window sill.[12]

To think of haymaking in the slums of Salford, and then to
carry the idea through, surely required an artist's inspiration
and determination? Whether it can be legitimate or appropriate
to use the word 'art' for such a thing would be questioned by
some — at the time such usage would certainly have seemed
bizarre — yet recent developments in visual art, as a result of
which one would not be the least bit surprised if an artist such
as Richard Long built a haycock in an art gallery, suggest the
possibility of a comparison between Mrs Roberts' haymaking
and contemporary 'installations' and 'land art'.

The doll's house, sometimes home-made, is not only a world
within a world but a home within a home. Like model worlds of
all kinds, it appeals to our delight in miniaturization; it offers us
the two possibilities of playing at gods, peering down on, or
peering into, a tiny world that is ours to control, or imagining
ourselves small so that we can enter and inhabit it. Miniature
worlds of these kinds offer precisely the kind of — safe — way out
of the home, into a — in a sense — larger world, referred to earlier
in this chapter; this interpretation is confirmed and illustrated
by the way in which this idea has been explored in children's
literature where, either by being plunged straight into the
world inhabited by tiny beings,[13] or by engaging with a model
or other world through a child hero or heroine, the reader is
taken beyond the stage of playing at gods with inert figures, to
encountering authentic personalities and problems that are not
so easy to resolve:[14] whatever the outcome, closing the book
offers instant passage home! But also, attending to what is
small and close-to (which can be done directly), or by seeing
through the eyes of someone who *is* tiny and low down, can
enrich one's sense of what is real; it is possible to switch from
an *imaginative* and childlike mode of perception, as in Robert
Louis Stevenson's 'My kingdom':

107

Down by a shining water well
I found a very little dell,
No higher than my head.
The heather and the gorse about
In summer bloom were coming out,
Some yellow and some red.

I called the little pool a sea
The little hills were big to me.
For I am very small.
I made a boat, I made a town,
I searched the caverns up and down,
And named them one and all . . .[15]

to observation, as recorded by Gerald Durrell:

This doll's house garden was a magic land, a forest of flowers
through which roamed creatures I had never seen before.

There was a whole landscape on this wall if you peered closely
enough to see it; the roofs of a hundred tiny toadstools, red,
yellow, and brown, showed in patches like villages on the
damper portions; a mountain of bottle-green moss grew in
tuffets so symmetrical that they might have been planted and
trimmed; forests of small ferns sprouted from cracks in the
shady places, drooping languidly like little green fountains.[16]

Using miniature worlds as a lens may thus provide vital exercise
in perception, encouraging a facility for slipping easily from
macrocosm to microcosm and back again, enabling us to see a
'world in a grain of sand'.

Christmas has its own miniature world, that of the crib, a
homely world in spite of the homelessness of its human inhabitants. Our own crib of several Christmases, assembled from a
kit comprising cardboard cut-outs, benefits from being lit, like
the Roberts' Greek temple, by a night light in a darkened room;
one Christmas the sheep and donkey were joined by a plastic
dinosaur (not to scale) and a clockwork mouse, who looked on
with due reverence and immediately seemed to belong. Within
the family, the same figures, rediscovered by eager hands each

Christmas Eve and lovingly arranged and re-arranged, are also loved because they are so much a part of the family's own tradition, of a world and a continuity which can be utterly relied on.

10

Gardens

On Sunday, we took a bottle of wine and went up to their allotment. Sitting up on the hill overlooking the sea . . . drinking . . . talking. The allotment was made by a Greek and had been left the same — a series of secret gardens with box hedges, and a little hut with a mirror hanging in it and a tiny cupboard and . . . Greek family photographs.

Nell Dunn, *Living Like I Do*, 1977

Almost every aspect of family art — including its subversion or transformation of convention — can be illustrated by gardens. And yet, though part of the home and, often, especially beloved of children, the garden as family art is an elusive topic. Gardens are at once slow to mature and vulnerable to changes of ownership. The garden is not an artefact that a family can pack up and take with it (except in photographs). Even when relatively enclosed and situated at the rear of the house, smaller gardens are likely to be overlooked by neighbouring houses; few modest gardens are really private; allotment gardens — which in Europe and Scandinavia (or, in the case of the Brighton allotment described above, as created in England by European gardeners) are almost a second home, a weekend retreat for all the family, not just a vegetable plot — rub shoulders on the same parcel of land.[1] Gardens are thus relatively public, and in any case the 'language' of gardens does not lend itself to overt individual or family expression.

The history of the family garden does not appear to reach back beyond the beginning of the nineteenth century. Such a

110

conclusion appears to fit neatly enough with our observations on the history of the family, the family home, and of family art, but again, appearances should be treated with some caution:

> . . . I am assuming that the lack of evidence of pre-nineteenth-century democratic or popular ornamental gardens represents an absence of the type. Such reasoning from negative evidence is never secure, because so very often all cultural evidence of a given time or place is funnelled – *filtered* is a better term – through the eyes, minds, hands and pens of an exclusive class which often does not deign to notice popular phenomena, and is sometimes quite blind to the ways of the preponderance of humanity.[2]

The *pre*history of the family garden certainly includes the gardens of Dutch seventeenth-century town houses, 'the first clear instance of the middle-class ornamental garden'.[3] The growth of 'an independent middle-class, homeownership and a degree of wealth',[4] and, especially, of suburban as well as of urban life, brought about the development of the suburban garden or, for those marooned in areas of dense housing or confined to apartments, of allotments or 'leisure gardens' (the Danish *kolonihaven* or German *Schrebergarten*). Like the family house throughout the same period, the garden was and remains the subject of countless advisory books and magazines and, nowadays, of radio and television programmes; typically, these draw their aesthetics from other, grander, sources; they cite the example of small gardens selectively and according to their own criteria. The family garden as a *family* garden, that is, as unique to a particular family, has been comprehensively ignored.

In the nineteenth century in particular, much of the literature of exhortation and instruction was, like that of homemaking (and indeed as a growth of it) addressed to women; although not expected to perform any but the lighter, more delicate tasks involved, the lady of the house had a crucial role to play in bringing her moral superiority and aesthetic sensibilities to bear outdoors as well as in. 'As the house is Art-production, so is the garden that surrounds it',[5] writers on gardening insisted towards the end of the century. The modest garden has found it

111

Plate 16   *Gateway of a Danish 'kolonihaven'*. (Photograph: the author)

difficult to liberate itself entirely from the grandiose achievements of the well-to-do, except, as in the case of the allotment,
by removing itself from the house and residential area altogether.
Many styles and features of 'popular' gardening can be traced
to elevated sources: formal, oriental, and 'picturesque' garden
design have influenced small gardens, whereas the evolution of
an independent and original style of garden design in England
by, most notably, William Robinson and Gertrude Jekyll,
although inspired by natural scenery and by humble cottage
gardens, depended on the creation of by no means minuscule
gardens for relatively well-off patrons, before becoming
another source of inspiration for small and suburban gardens.
Even such apparently quirky features as rockeries and garden

112

gnomes have an illustrious ancestry, and many garden ornaments are the outdoor parallels of the pathetic imitations of
grandeur exposed by Peter Lloyd-Jones:[6]

> Gnomes and dwarfs; concrete toadstools painted with white
> spots on a lurid red background; shoddy and ridiculously out-
> of-scale imitation well-heads, and concrete staddle-stones, have
> been manufactured by the thousands, and used to make count-
> less front gardens ridiculous. The essential ingredient of these
> ornaments is sentiment. . . . To this end they must therefore
> imitate something familiar from the past . . .[7]

The trend continues: the opening up of country houses – in
Britain, especially through the agency of the National Trust – has
enabled thousands of small-scale gardeners to wander the
paths of magnificent stately gardens, which have thus been
confirmed in their role as inspiration and archetype.

The *public* aspect of gardens means that experimentation will
excite curiosity (and maybe, disapproval), and that failures
cannot be hidden, and may take time to redeem. In suburban
areas, the garden, especially the lawn, takes the place of, for
example, the scrubbed pavements and donkey-stoned door
step of working-class housing in the towns of northern
England, as *the* touchstone of social acceptability. My father,
who could not bear to mow flowering daisies (and mowed
around them), was Wordsworthian in his recognition of natural
beauty not least in its least assuming forms; nor would he have
compromised that recognition for the sake of some silly convention that insists that a lawn should be daisy-less and as smooth
and green as a billiard table. But to innovate in the garden can
require no little courage! Some of the most strenuous, bold and
in some cases, bizarre attempts to break away into something
completely different, are most typically the work of original,
eccentric individuals rather than of families. In such cases it is
again the *public* aspect of the garden which has stimulated, not
conformity, but open defiance, a deliberate and self-conscious
show intended to attract attention; even where part of the
motivation may be to delight children with sculpted shapes and
grottoes, or model landscapes, such gardens tend to leave little

room for children to develop them or to participate except on terms dictated by the garden.[8]

But there is scope in gardening for the spirit of family art. By and large, the materials of gardening, including the site, are *given* and embody their own possibilities; creation is a matter of choosing from, and making use of, what is available. Yet the range of choice is considerable, and the interpretation of and variations on themes can be bold and innovative. Thus *a garden can be created which reflects individual traits and treasured memories not apparent to the uninitiated*. For example, at the time of writing this I am trying to grow a mixed patch of two wild flowers, scabious and knapweed. My father, who died last year, loved to see these two flowers flourishing together among the grass of chalk landscapes. They may not take to the clay of this garden, but one wild flower that has established itself, ramsons, through its sight and scent recalls several springtime holidays that my wife and I enjoyed years ago. At Sissinghurst in Kent, Harold Nicolson and Vita Sackville-West created a garden that was the ground of their marriage, a lover's-knot, a gift that they constantly gave to one another and that has endured to become the most visited garden in England. It is not small (though much smaller than the estate Vita had grown up in and expected to inherit); nor is it startlingly, radically innovative, or obviously peculiar to its makers, in that it accepts and breathes its own life into established languages of gardening. Yet it blends and quietly articulates different preferences:

> In Sissinghurst's creating Vita had indelibly stamped her romantic personality . . . on the courtyard . . . in the Rondel Rose Garden and in the orchard. Harold's classicism . . . rules the Lombardy poplared entrance, his Lime Walk, the Nuttery and the Yew Walk. That these elements combine with such harmony is the measure of their complementary souls . . .[9]

Thus the garden can embody personal and familial preferences and memories and to this limited extent, can *portray* individuals and families. In addition it can be designed to *meet a family's practical requirements and to respond to, and thus reflect, the*

114

family's way of life. This can include growing vegetables and herbs for the table (the family will have its own favourites), or flowers to be cut (and perhaps dried) for the house. It is likely to include *provision for children* — not just an area of grass to play on but also, places for dens, small ponds and wildernesses for nature study, a model railway, a generous sand-pit,[10] and a tea-kitchen[11] or other facilities for cooking outdoors. I was recently astonished to see, in a Danish *kolonihaven*, two sets of football posts complete with nets, the two together virtually enclosing an area of grass to make the smallest football pitch imaginable amid a wealth of flowers and vegetables. Garden and outbuildings can also, of course, accommodate various hobbies and crafts, the products of which — windmills, windvanes, wrought iron gates — may embellish and add their own idiosyncratic touch to the garden itself.

In these ways, then, a garden can be shaped by a family around their own unique identity, rather than merely imitating other gardens; in the process, it begins to say something about them to the visitor and the passer-by, and what it says is more than a bland statement to the effect that the family is doing very nicely, thank you, and is accepted within its neighbourhood and social class. In its role as mediator between the private, enclosed world of home and the wider world beyond, the garden can be cultivated as a device for *extending hospitality and expressing neighbourliness.* That is to say, rather than employing it as a disguise to pretend that the family is the same as other families (and therefore of little interest), the family uses the garden to say 'Welcome' in a way that is friendly but is at the same time unashamedly an expression of that family. This is well illustrated by European *kolonihaver,* each discrete group of which flourishes as a community with a degree of communal organization, shared resources, often an area of common ground (usually incorporating play equipment), and communal events (notably an annual competition), for these are communities that thrive on their endless differences and that produce innumerable variations on a theme. As an outside room the garden may be used for entertaining visitors, and — as also happens inside — here the visitor may begin to interpret and enter into dialogue with the family's articulating of itself through 'family art'. Where the garden is especially open to view, it can be conceived as a contribution to the neighbourhood, intended to give pleasure: in this context it is only reasonable to take account of the overall character of the neighbourhood. This tendency may be particularly strong in North America, where a tradition of open gardens can be traced back to 'the *clearing*, which expands outward . . .',[12] and where 'The popular democratic garden . . . seems to be designed to please the visitor and the passerby quite as much as the resident.'[13]

Finally, a garden may be cultivated *in order to enlarge the 'family' and to complete the 'world' of home*. Pets are members of the family, and some pets need gardens. (Conversely, some gardens need pets. 'My garden would not be half the pleasure it is to me without the pussies', wrote Gertrude Jekyll, who devoted a chapter of her book *Children and gardens* to this topic.[14]) Deceased pets are sometimes buried in gardens, with due ceremony and in suitably marked graves. A garden completes home as a microcosm of the world, for even a modest garden is a landscape of sorts, a habitat, an ecological community; if it is large enough for a wild corner to be acceptable, the number of species will multiply, and its potential interest and educative value will increase accordingly.

11

Hospitality and Community

There can be no doubt that the cult of family can be taken too far. Consider Edward Shorter's characterization of the 'modern' family:

> Secluded behind closed shutters from outside, members of the family spin about themselves that web of sentiment the French allude to as *chacun chez soi* . . .[1]

And he describes the coming into being of the modern family as a transition from 'household' — which might contain grandparents, other relatives, servants, farm hands, apprentices — to 'nest'. Robert Roberts recalls that one of the mottoes that appeared in lower working-class homes in the last century was 'Home is the Nest where all is Best',[2] and Ruskin, writing in 1867, used the phrase 'Art of the Nest' to describe the then current vogue for painting pictures of domestic scenes. Indeed, we still talk of children, when they grow up, 'leaving the nest', a phrase that at least admits to the existence of life outside the nest.

To a degree, the metaphor is appropriate enough: the family home *does* provide for the transition between womb and world; but for the children's sake not least it is vital that it should not be entirely 'secluded behind closed shutters'. Over-emphasis on family privacy causes *neighbourhood* and *community* to atrophy, generating a vicious circle in which families are forced back even more on themselves, into isolation and competition. What is needed, then, is more interaction between families, and within

117

local communities seen as larger families; that this is the natural orientation for families is demonstrated by Csikszentmihalyi and Rochberg-Halton whose research revealed that:

> . . . those who freely give their attention to their family to create a warm home ultimately have a richer, more diverse public life as well.[3]

Csikszentmihalyi and Rochberg-Halton do not dissent from Shorter's analysis of the development of the modern family; indeed they illuminate it by contrasting the 'classical bourgeois family . . . held together by the heavy weight of social traditions' with contemporary, successful (i.e. happy and 'warm') families which are 'practically *invented* by their members':

> Outside constraints are relatively light; the meanings that keep these families together are woven and mended by the constant attention of those who comprise them.[4]

But such caring and commitment will not and cannot be confined within the family, and thus traditional critics of the family are confounded:

> Paradoxically, these warm families seem to accomplish exactly what Marxist and Freudian theoriticians hoped the abolition of the bourgeois family would accomplish: a greater involvement and integration in the community. . . . On this score the traditional family arrangement seems to draw on a deeper source of wisdom than many modern theories, which have run afoul of human nature in trying to instill communal goals in children by short-circuiting the family . . .[5]

Family art is not solely concerned with decking-out the home as a sealed-off nest; it is certainly not devoted to creating a jack-daw's nest embellished with the glint and glitter of consumer goods. It contributes rather to creating the home as a microcosm of the world that gently leads into and opens windows onto the world: a home that can incorporate stones and shells from the beach, plants tended in the house or brought in from the garden, or a garden that might typically proceed through stages of relative tidiness and order to a wild corner; all of these offer connections between home and the vast, awesome world of Nature, for example. This could not be more eloquently illustrated than by the words of an 8-year-old boy, asked what his 'special objects' meant to him:

> They make me feel like I'm part of the world. . . . Because when I look at them, I keep my eyes on them and I think what they mean. Like I have a bank from the First National, and when I look at it I think what it means. It means money for our cities and our country, it means tax for the government. My stuffed bunny reminds me of wildlife, all the rabbits, and dogs and cats. That toy animal over there [a plastic lion] reminds me of circuses and the way they train animals so that they don't get hurt. That's what I mean, all my special things make me feel like I'm part of the world.[6]

Pets adopted into the family introduce an element of *otherness*, mysterious embodiments of a larger world; they are a constant reminder, within the home, of the limits of domestication. Thus a cat, coming in and going out as and when it chooses, is a living shuttle threading itself betwixt and between the warp of cosy domesticity (which it appreciates as much as anyone) and the weft of outdoors, Nature, night. Maybe too this reflecting and echoing between domestic and wider worlds explains something of the fascination of the 'miniature' worlds of Lego, toy farms, and model railways; here, in the relatively small world of home, is a larger world made smaller than a single room.

In making a world within the world, family art constructs a world of its own in which a particular family feels especially at home, and that reflects that family's identity. This is just part of a process of making oneself, ourselves, at home in the world at large; it involves staking out 'private' territory, and as such it is also a public statement, but if that public statement says 'Private: Keep Out' then the process of making oneself at home in the world cannot be completed. Given such insecurity, one cannot expect even to feel 'at home' in the home, only marginally less fearful. Family art contributes to the making of home as a positive announcement of the family's identity that facilitates

119

interaction with the community and is capable of saying 'Welcome', and it does this through both exterior and interior.

The *exterior* of the home, visible to passers-by, can hardly avoid carrying some kind of message, whether by accident or design: family art can help it to be by design. In so doing it is likely to employ family variants of public languages, and possibly, to carry on longstanding civic traditions. The inhabitants of Dutch town houses of the seventeenth century, which as depicted in contemporary paintings are frequently seen, from the inside, to have a door standing open onto the street, extended their house-pride outside the house itself to include 'their' stretch of pavement: Vermeer's 'A street in Delft' clearly shows a servant washing the pavement in front of the house; also visible are the benches on which the family would sit in the late afternoon and early evening, conversing with their neighbours.[7] In their ceaseless cleansing of home and pavement Dutch housewives may be seen to have vigorously 'patrolled that dangerous frontier between the dirt of the street and the cleanliness of the home';[8] dirt represented everything beyond the home, vice not least, which could threaten domesticity. Yet at the same time the world of outdoors was 'not in the least threatening'.[9] In industrial England, and specifically in Preston (where I am writing this book),

> In front of each house were two or three stone flags which it was the custom of the housewives to wash and clean with 'donkey stones' each weekend, and at Easter time the door-jambs and lintels over the doors and windows had to be similarly treated. . . . Another Easter custom was to visit the cemetery on Thursday before Good Friday and scrub the gravestone.[10]

At Todmorden, the element of artistry was more apparent:

> Most people in the street took great pride in the appearance of their houses, especially the outsides. . . . The doorsteps were scoured with donkey stone, and the more houseproud the women were the more elaborate patterns edged the steps. Some preferred to make their patterns with yellow stone, which was the colour of yellow ochre. . . . On wash-days the streets were festooned with lines of washing . . . and there was fierce competition to have the cleanest washing in the street.[11]

120

Greek women in Yerania spend much of their mornings cleaning and doing domestic chores indoors, and sweep and sometimes mark out in whitewash an area of the pavement and street corresponding with the house-front and projecting to the middle of the road; in the afternoon they bring out a chair and sit crocheting or embroidering, at first facing inwards to their own front door then, as others come out too, a group is formed, more chairs are offered to passers-by, coffee and conversation are shared. In this way the stretch of pavement in front of the house

> takes on the aspect of the home, its barriers relaxed but not eradicated. It could be said that 'The house enters the street', for the chair, an item of *indoor* furnishing, is brought *outside*.[12]

There were, and are, other ways in which the exterior of the house (quite apart from a front garden) can convey specific messages. In Dutch towns, when a child was born, the family hung a *kraam kloppertje*, a small placard of wood or paper covered with red silk and trimmed with lace, on the doors of the house. 'This placard was a real family treasure';[13] the *kloppertjes*

> became yet another object of rich local ornamental variation: as elaborate and particularized as other domestic and civic fetishes, like the drinking horn or the bonnet pin. Moreover, the posting of the *kloppertje*, along with the father's donning the paternity bonnet, announced a period when the household would be exempt from certain taxes and duties. So the birth was very much a semipublic and neighbourhood event, with innumerable parties and feasts marking the earliest calendar of the child.[14]

Into this century the vanes of Dutch windmills, by themselves or augmented with flags or other trimmings, fixed in one or other of a variety of positions, were used to make very public statements to the surrounding area, and indeed messages were passed in this way from windmill to windmill: the language of the windmill announced births, marriages, and deaths, including, of course, such events in the life of the miller's own family.[15]

Doors, but also windows, are the openings through which

'the house enters the street' and vice-versa. At Christmas, we hang Christmas wreaths on our front doors, and place Christmas trees in our windows, leaving the curtains undrawn. In present-day Holland, curtains are left undrawn as a matter of course all year round, and windows are filled with a display of house plants and perhaps other things, through which the interior may be glimpsed. The windows of contemporary Danish homes are frequently decorated on the inside with pictures and patterns, cut out in card in tinted silhouette and hung from a thread, perhaps more often bought than home-made but clearly intended to catch the eye of passer-by and visitor although also giving pleasure when seen from within. A curious painting by Oluf Braren, 'Private wedding on the island of Föhr'[16] of c. 1800–25, graphically visualizes the interplay of private and public aspects of the wedding, which in local custom could take place in private homes but not to the exclusion of the community. Thus the nearest relatives assemble in the house, and other guests gather outside and look through the windows. Braren's painting represents the wedding as seen from outside – the canvas is divided into four, corresponding to four windowpanes, while the openness of the house is further emphasized by the open doors at the back of the room, leading through a succession of open doors to the street beyond.

When visitors are invited *into* the home, family art can enhance hospitality, in two ways. First, by helping the interior of the home to articulate the family, thus introducing them to guests and 'breaking the ice'. Secondly, by making home homely, family art makes it the more homely for both family and guests, thus helping the latter to feel 'at home'. Both aspects of hospitality, are illustrated by the Danish concept of *hygge*, which, strictly untranslatable, means something like 'homeliness' – a quality, that is, derived from, but not exclusively associated with, the home.[17] (In fact, the Danish language distinguishes between *hygge* in general, and *hjemlig hygge* or homely *hygge* in particular.) *Hygge* can perhaps be defined as that sense of well-being which arises from feeling 'at home'; shelter and physical comfort are prerequisites, but feeling at home requires more than that. It is above all a feeling of belonging in one's own right, in familiar or friendly surroundings, in good company, and thus in circumstances which mirror, confirm, and bring out one's best self. A sense of familiarity is essential − a strange environment can convey this especially if its familiarity to its own people has been cultivated by them to produce a *quality* of familiarity to which others can readily respond. This is more likely to have happened over a period of time, and a vital element is likely to be represented by 'minder' (redefined to include other things besides memorial inscriptions):

> A *minde* is a keepsake, a souvenir, a memento; it is a reminder of past experience. . . . A *minde* is a treasure, brought out period-ically to be fondled and enjoyed anew. Encapsulation of present experience intensifies the present moment with an awareness that it will be tomorrow's memory. Thus scrapbooks and photo-graphic records of 'memorable' occasions are virtually universal in Danish households and [are] frequently consulted, tangible expressions of the interplay between past and present. More-over, slides and home movies are often shown in contexts associated with *hygge*. Serving as a symbol of experiences shared with other participants or as a 'conversation-piece' for sharing in the present moment, these visual records are used to enhance the sense of embeddedness with which viewers invest their relationships to one another.[18]

Crucially, some 'minder' remain visible in the home so that

> an entering visitor is immediately aware of the personal−historic atmosphere of the living space. A room without these accretions is uninviting, both because it is impersonal and because it suggests a lack of involvement on the part of the inhabitant with common human experiences . . .[19]

Although certain qualities are *un-hyggelig* − as for instance, newness, extreme tidiness, or extremes of any kind − and in spite of the fact that Danish women's and family magazines *do* concern themselves with *hygge*, it is generally acknowledged that *hygge* is not attained by conforming to rules of 'home-making' or a strict aesthetic: not only is it too subtle and elusive for that, but also its one rule, so to speak, is to take no notice of anything that would inhibit or restrict personal and familial creativity and independence of expression:

> . . . It is more *hyggelig* to sit in a living room which is clearly being lived in than in a perfectly appointed living room such as might be found in a furniture exhibition.[20]

While *hygge* can be found and relished on one's own, on a small scale, it is most commonly associated with togetherness, on a small scale, when it is a feeling of being at home *with others*. And it is elusive, in that, although a good deal can be done to consciously create the conditions in which *hygge* can thrive, it is 'a fickle guest which comes when it suits it and most often when no one has called for it':[21] Danish people will go to endless trouble to prepare a dinner party and help their guests feel at home − invoking not only *hygge* but also *festlighed*, making the occasion *festive* − but ultimately much depends on chance and on the chemistry of interpersonal relations (rather as the successful giving of a gift depends for its completion on the recipient).

On such occasions, domesticity becomes almost a religion; a shared celebration of values; an invocation of the *spirit* of those values. (That domesticity and religion can converge will be seen in the course of the next chapter). In this context − as in religious rites, to which participants bring their private concerns, their families, themselves − there need be no conflict between personal and social, private and public: the one depends on the other; there can be no community without individuality. Thus the language of family art is not entirely idiosyncratic; it is not merely a secret code confined to each family; indeed, something of the language of homeliness, of *hygge*, can be employed outside the home itself, as for example in the 'homely' surroundings of an inn or restaurant. On the one hand, even at its most private, family art may not be wholly opaque to the stranger who will most readily feel at home in a strange house which is clearly an *authentic* home: from even its most private elements, family art elaborates and articulates a widely understood if not a universal language. On the other hand, it draws on, extends hospitality to, and itself nourishes, communal expression and tradition: art — including folk art — that reflects the shared values, common heritage, and cultural identity of a community (local, regional, ethnic, religious, national), can in this wider sense be thought of as 'family art', and may produce much loved images which find their way into many homes. Portraits of royal families are a case in point, notably in countries like the United Kingdom, the Netherlands, or Denmark, where the monarch is regarded affectionately as the head of a nationwide family. Similarly, the widespread use of a national flag — as in Denmark, where it flies above gardens and appears on Christmas trees — can be familial and welcoming rather than aggressively patriotic. Devotional imagery likewise constitutes a kind of 'family art' linking religious communities. The more than a hundred interpretations of 'A peaceable kingdom' painted by Edward Hicks, an American untutored artist and a Quaker, were the result of a personal obsession with and, perhaps, a conscious or unconscious wish to propagate into universal acceptance, a vision of a homelike world, a recreation of Paradise. A ubiquitous image, which does not reflect a local, regional, national, or religious so much as a broadly European or just plain human hankering for a Paradise lost, is that of a pastoral landscape, after the style of Claude or Poussin: its wide appeal must surely be explained in terms of a yearning to feel 'at home' in a benign universe, rather than as a universal wish to inhabit a land precisely as depicted and complete with Classical ruins.[22]

In its fusion of private and public; in its lending of itself to welcoming and sharing; in its articulating and celebrating of domestic, secular values that are at one with our aspirations to feel at home in the universe and to welcome the very spirit of the universe into our domestic bliss, the bosom of our family, the language of family art is supremely a language of hospitality and community.

12

Letting in Infinity

The house has not invariably been regarded simply as a device for keeping the outside out, and indeed in some cultural traditions it is conceived as an echo of the cosmos, the floor representing earth, the ceiling sky, and so forth – a way of seeing which facilitates perception of the infinite as 'home' without diminishing it.[1] For many families within different societies and traditions, home is a spiritual abode, a place of contemplation and celebration; if the house itself is not conceived in explicitly cosmic terms, it may nonetheless contain votive images. In Greek homes, for instance, there is invariably an *iconostasi*, a shelf with icons in front of which is suspended an oil-lamp that is lit each evening, or on Saturday evenings, or at major religious festivals. 'Each house in Yerania is a religious community . . .'.[2] Some comparable arrangement or the presence of icons or votive pictures is commonplace in other countries and traditions; or else, as with the Quakers, no one corner, no particular images, are invested with especial spiritual values but the whole home in its every aspect is regarded in a sacramental light. (In Greek and other traditions it is the woman of the house who is the family's priestess and creative spirit: the one who tends the sacred images and the home itself, the one who is 'intercessor for her family, caring for the spiritual needs of both living and dead members'.[3])

Seen in this light, homemaking, and the work of family art, is a bringing of blessings to the home, an invoking of guardian angels, a making of a heaven on earth, a fulfilment of prophecy

126

('Then my people shall live in a tranquil country, dwelling in peace, in houses full of ease'[4]). It is part of a process of making a home *in which divinity is a presence* – as represented, for example, by the Christ child in the Christmas crib, by the images of Christ incorporated in the visual aspect of the home (as in Aran or Greek interiors), and by the *spirit* invoked by domestic religious observances. Even if we cannot embrace the certainty of faith, home is the place wherein those we love most especially are gathered, and we come near to prayer in our constant care that it, and they, should remain safe from harm.

The Jewish faith is probably the most home-oriented of all major religions. Two aspects of Jewish domestic religious practice are worth stressing in particular. First, that, perhaps surprisingly, and in spite of the existence of an extraordinary inheritance of rules or laws (indeed, partly because so many rules necessitate both choice and interpretation), there is scope to innovate; indeed, creativity is at the heart of Jewish faith and practice. Secondly, that Jewish customs involve a rich and diverse interaction between private and public spheres, between family and community (and indeed, a whole people).

Jewish reverence for the home is illustrated by the traditional story, retold by Martin Buber, of Rabbi Eizik, who after many years of poverty dreamed that he was bidden to look for treasure in Prague under the bridge that leads to the king's palace. When he got there, he found the bridge was guarded, so that he could not dig, but when he told the captain of the guard about his dream, the captain replied:

> 'As for having faith in dreams, if I had had it, I should have had to get going when a dream once told me to go to Cracow and dig for treasure under the stove in the room of a Jew – Eizik, son of Yekel, that was the name! Eizik, son of Yekel! I can just imagine what it would be like, how I should have to try every house over there, where one half of the Jews are named Eizik and the other Yekel!'[5]

And of course, Eizik promptly went home and dug up the treasure! Theologically, the Jewish faith is founded on the family – and by the same token, on creativity – in that God is

127

regarded as having deliberately left Creation incomplete, so that it can be continued through human procreation and (in a broad and profound sense, which anticipates the following chapter) home-making. Jewish religious observance and its calendar of festivals structures both the week and the year, as well as marking and celebrating individual 'rites of passage' through a lifetime; worship takes place as much if not more in the home than in the synagogue, in some cases focusing very much on the home, and in several ways.

This is true not least of Shabbat, the Sabbath, the formally observed weekly day of rest that therefore becomes a celebration of home as the place of rest. What people rest from is (or should be) the task of Creation; *domestic* creativity reaches a weekly climax in preparations for the Shabbat. Special *challah* bread is made; the table is set, with candles in candlesticks and the challah plate in readiness. Shabbat begins at sunset on Friday; the candles are lit and blessed, traditionally by the woman of the home; the father invokes a blessing on the children; the singing of the Kiddush (a blessing of the wine and a thanksgiving for the Sabbath) and the blessing of the bread initiate the Shabbat meal. The candlesticks are likely to be one of the family's most treasured possessions, very much a *minde* and as likely as not an heirloom cherished through difficult times:

> The story we all loved best, and beseeched her time and again to retell, explained how the brass candlesticks we use every Friday night happen to be on our table (and provided us with a kind of capsule history of how countless Jews and pairs of candlesticks came to the United States).
>
> In the mid-1880s life was difficult for Grandma's family in Russia; economic problems were complicated by the fact that her teen-age brothers would soon be eligible for the Czar's army, in which Jews regularly suffered severe discrimination and mistreatment. Her parents, Moses and Molly Katchuk, finally planned to escape with their eight children.
>
> They were able to take little with them but the clothes they wore, and knapsacks with a couple of changes for each person — only what was necessary and could easily be carried. As they prepared to leave their home for ever, Grandma remembered

her mother gathering her brood to her, holding the baby in one arm while clutching the Shabbat candlesticks with her free hand. Then they fled.[6]

This account is taken from *Jewish family celebrations* by Arlene Rossen Cardozo, a book on which I have drawn heavily in writing this chapter and that sets out to share, joyously and in a very practical sense too, what one family gained by becoming more actively involved in Jewish observances. They did so by gradually assimilating and recreating those practices that they felt comfortable with; the spirit in which they approached tradition, and the scope for creative change, is illustrated by the author's statement that:

> in our family we *all* do the work and *all* enjoy the preparation for Shabbat and festivals, whereas in previous times it was the wife and mother who did the preparation, while the rest of the family enjoyed the celebration.[7]

Weddings, which mark the beginning of a new family and the founding of a new home, involve the use of a *chuppah*, a temporary construction of four posts covered with fabric, which recalls the tents of nomadic Jews while clearly also looking forward to the house that the couple are to make home, for here the groom waits for his bride. Not dissimilarly, the annual festival of Sukkot involves families in making and decorating temporary dwellings adjacent to their houses, again recalling nomadic life; whereas this is done partly in obedience to Jewish laws, and although basic plans and even prefabricated sukkahs may be available, there is ample scope for the sukkah to become a notable example of family art, a dwelling which the family makes, decorates, and – for a few days, at least at some meal-times, weather permitting – inhabits.

Typically, the sukkah is constructed from a wooden frame (which may be taken down and re-used year after year), free-standing or a lean-to against the house, to which branches or (where available) maize stalks or other natural material (known generically as *sekhakh*) are attached. The sukkah provides shade, but gaps must be left in the roof so that the stars can be seen. Further embellishment can be added in the form of leaves, fruits, or gourds:

> . . . we use gourds rather than fresh fruit since our Minnesota squirrels are oblivious to the rabbinical injunction that sukkah decorations are not to be eaten during the festival.[8]

Arlene Rossen Cardozo describes how her family designed and built a hexagonal sukkah:

> Our sukkah frame is an example of putting one's own touches on an ancient tradition, for never before had we ever heard of, or seen anything but a rectangular sukkah. In fact, at first I was very self-conscious about our 'different sukkah'. Was it really all right? A couple of years after Dick designed ours, some friends built a similar but much more elaborate round sukkah.
>
> Recently a new rabbi moved to town and [we] invited him over during Sukkot. Afterwards, he remarked, 'How interesting, the Jews of Minnesota build round sukkot'. This, I suspect, is how new interpretations of old customs are born![9]

For virtually all Jewish celebrations, particular food is specially prepared, and we should not lose sight of the element of cretivity, and indeed of family art, in the developing and refining of recipes, in the shaping of dough into (sometimes) symbolic form, and in the ritual of the meal lit by candles and accompanied by blessings. Sukkot is no exception:

> We usually invite close friends to share the fun of the first night of Sukkot with us. As we gather in our newly gourd-squash-pumpkin-decorated, cornstalk-walled hut, we precede the meal with the lighting of the festival candles; the festival Kiddush; the Shehecheyanu; the blessing of the sukkah, *lulav* and *etrog*; and the blessing over the bread.[10]

Surely even non-Jewish Danes would recognize the Jewish genius for creating their own version of *hygge*?

Family art may also be in evidence in, for example, the making of Hanukkah candle holders (Hanukkah is a festival of light, at which one candle is lit for each person):

> in our house we now use several hanukiyot each Hannukah as, in addition to lighting our own candles, we kindle lights for

Soviet Jewish families who may not be free to do so themselves. So each year we utilize our many home-crafted hanukiyot, some of which have lasted but one season and some for many. One of our favourites is a painted flat board; glued to it are walnut shells, which serve as candleholders. We've also made some unusual hanukiyot of clay . . .[11]

Modest gifts may take the place of the traditional Hanukkah *gelt* – coins given to each child on one or all nights of Hanukkah; some families value home-made gifts above all.[12] Wedding gifts can include a hand-made *ketubah* or marriage certificate, the work of a Jewish calligrapher. 'Their own ketubah is perhaps the most visually magnificent and meaningful gift a couple will ever receive'.[13] The festival of Shavuot, a kind of spring harvest festival, is marked by decorating the house with flowers, transforming it into 'an indoor garden'. Other festivals may be the occasion of family theatricals, as when Purim is marked by re-enacting the story of Esther,[14] and the Passover by recalling and maybe dramatizing the Exodus out of Egypt.

Whereas Jewish families celebrate in their own home and (working within and reinterpreting tradition and Jewish law) in their own way, they do not do so in isolation. Celebrations in the home and in the synagogue constantly echo one another; at the same time, virtually all the time (although especially at certain times) the home is open to the extended family and to Jewish friends and neighbours who will join in ritual meals and ceremonies. The Jewish New Year, like Christmas for many Christians, has become a time to send out greetings cards to distant friends and relatives; Yom Kippur, shortly after, is a time both for healing any disunity within the family and also for forgiveness, reconciliation, and renewal in the wider network of relationships centred on the synagogue. Weddings, births, name days, Bar Mitzvah and Bat Mitzvah, and other ceremonies of 'rites of passage' all have a strong public dimension; during the first seven, intense days of mourning, the mourners remain at home and are visited by friends and relatives who will also bring and serve food so that the mourners are relieved of the task of preparing meals. But also, all Jewish customs, some explicitly so, link the family not merely with the local Jewish community but with the whole Jewish people and their history. This is clearly true, for instance, of the Passover; more recent and sombre events are commemorated at Yom Hasho'ah, the day set aside each year for remembering the Holocaust.

The home-based yet community-orientated nature of Jewish rite and custom, and more generally, the way in which families can meet and share through creativity, is beautifully symbolized by a recollection of spending Shavuot in Jerusalem,

> a time when Israeli families sit around the table, singing for hours. Balcony windows are all open, and the strains of one family's songs joins with another until the whole street is filled with music. In fact, a family in one apartment may start a song, and families in other neighbouring apartments join in so that many persons who may never really socialize with one another end up singing together.[15]

Like any religion, the Jewish faith represents a transaction between humanity and the Infinite; in part by means of its rules and rituals, it ensures that every stage of life, every day, and virtually every moment are 'observed', and thus it makes religion constant, a way of life; it explicitly links family and home with cosmos and Heaven. Whereas the family invokes the presence and blessings of God directly, it does so through ancient forms of words and through rituals drawn from a common tradition; it inherits a body of belief and an accumulation of rules. It might be argued that any religion, not least religions that are continually reaffirmed by many members, *protects* people from the kind of direct, existential contact with a possibly empty infinity that can bring a shiver to one's soul under a night sky or in vast, comfortless places; some would say that the elaboration and multiplication of laws and rituals by the Jewish people can only be explained as the building of a wall to hide behind, a structuring of life so that there is no room for infinity to get in. No doubt this can be true of many religions, when their adherents adopt them as a habit; the faith of those of whatever faith, who are always prepared to work on their faith, to test it, and to ceaselessly recreate it, demands respect from believer and disbeliever alike. What can be said with some certainty is that a family's religious observances, particularly in the form of rituals in the home, contribute significantly to the 'world' that parents construct around their children:

> Each year . . . I realize how much children love custom; how much the rituals of holiday preparation and celebration are an integral part of them, and of their security; and how much richer their futures will be for the memories of the past, which these treasured moments so shortly become.[16]

While religious domestic practices can be beneficial to young children, the faith of the parents can (but perhaps need not) be problematic and a cause of distress later on; sooner or later the growing children have to confront the nature of religious belief as faith, not fact, and either embrace it as their own faith, or discard it. I can certainly remember some pain associated with this process; although my parents did nothing to add to the pain, I found myself wishing that they and perhaps more particularly other religious instructors I had been exposed to had distinguished more clearly between faith and fact; yet I am conscious that much of the happiness I recall from childhood and associate particularly with the celebration of Christmas had a lot to do with the comforting nature of religious certainties. In our own practice as parents, we are trying to leave more room for our children to work out their own convictions in, without denying any possibilities and without setting out to confront or undermine the religious education they receive at school. And yet we have fostered belief in Father Christmas for all it is worth! Of course, these considerations are taking us outside the scope of this book, except insofar as creativity may be a key: religious faith (or whatever takes its place) is, in a sense, something we must all create or recreate for ourselves, making use of available material as we wish; by the same token, we should not impose our faith on others, but we may make what we have made available, and we will naturally wish to do so for our own children.

Religion, then, can be comforting and 'homely', rather than being challenging; but it can also be and indeed essentially *is*

133

comforting *and challenging* at the same time. *Hygge* involves feeling safe and secure, cosy, and enclosed; *home* is quintessentially a safe and enclosed place. Yet, paradoxically perhaps, home can open directly onto the infinite – as when in reflecting us, familiar objects sometimes seem to reveal hidden depths both in us and in themselves; or as in the elusiveness of *hygge* that in this respect has about it something of the mystery of a genie, confined in yet not confined by a small vessel, subject to being summoned and yet ultimately beyond human control. (The formal preparations undertaken by Danes in anticipation of a hospitable evening somehow remind me not only of Jewish practice, but also, of the setting-out of chairs and flowers in the Quaker Meeting House, and of the extreme care that goes into the making of a Japanese tea-house and into the tea ceremony. Neither is an end in itself nor a guarantee that the end in view will be fully realized.)

For Lucy Boston this aspect of home is illustrated by her inhabiting of a very old house, the Green Knowe of her children's books:

> It was like nowhere else, because while most houses are built to shut out everything but the inmates, to close doors and draw curtains equally against the cold winds from the edge of space and the curiosity of neighbours, to make a cosy den where everything is yours and under your control, Green Knowe was full of mysteries. Certainly it was welcoming and comfortable and rejoicing and gay, but one had the feeling that behind the exciting colours and shapes of its ancient self there might be surprises from the unknown universe; that the house was on good terms with that too, and had no intention of shutting out the un-understandable. Of course, it was largely Time. Surely Now and Not-now is the most teasing of all mysteries, and if you let in a nine-hundred-year dose of time, you let in almost everything.[17]

Similarly, yet dissimilarly also, Martin Buber gives the Jewish answer to the question 'Where is the dwelling of God?':

> 'God dwells wherever man lets him in'.
> This is the ultimate purpose: to let God in. But we can let him in only where we really stand, where we live, where we live a

true life. If we maintain holy intercourse with the little world entrusted to us, if we help the holy spiritual substance to accomplish itself in that section of Creation in which we are living, then we are establishing, in this our place, a dwelling for the Divine Presence.[18]

There, for those who can embrace it, is a complete theology of family art, for one can hardly admit the Creator and deny creativity. Csikszentmihalyi and Rochberg-Halton write of a 'cosmic self' in all of us that yearns to make sense, not just of what is immediately around us, but of 'the universe, the cosmos'.[19] And indeed, there is no paradox: the walls of home exist not to protect us from infinity but to *mediate* infinity; home provides us with a secure base to stand on, from which to contemplate the infinite without fear. In family art, as in other art, we engage in dialogue with the laws of the universe – birth, life, death; we extend the hospitality of our homes to God of whatever name, and endeavour to make of them a heaven on earth that embraces Infinity, a microcosm of a world that we would also make home, a haven of domestic bliss.

13

Giving and Perceiving

Familiarity is said to breed contempt; perhaps paradoxically, then, family art is the creating of a familiar environment that fosters *love* — love of home and the things around us, not least for their reassuring familiarity, and love of the people and memories we associate with them. Family art makes of the home an environment that can be taken for granted much of the time, as the practicalities of everyday life require, but which, loyal and dependable, is there when needed and fulfils particular needs by, for example, *coming into view* in comforting and reassuring ways. This can happen without prompting or intention — in a moment of relaxation our seeing strays, then comes to rest on this or that object when, before we know where we are, we are in the midst of recollections of an event in our lives, or maybe we are suffused with feelings of contentment and well-being. But something similar can be brought about more or less intentionally, not least through ceremonies that draw attention to certain things (like grace before a meal) or that (as in the case of birthdays) highlight particular members of the family. At Christmas, for example, we may transform much or all of the house, not covering up but embellishing its familiarity, so that we cannot help but see it anew. In these ways familiar things can become, suddenly 'for their moment the top of the world' (in Emerson's words). Family art's recreating of the domestic world around us — a means of 'comforting' and confirming ourselves — offers resources and strategies for communicating and sharing, for recreating the whole world as

136

'home' . . . and for transforming commerce and materialism in the process. And at the heart of all this, nourished within but overflowing out of the family, is the notion of giving and of the gift, an ability to see things *as if they are given* — as if they carry that additional charge of significance, over and above what they actually, literally, or merely are, which is present in a gift (and in all family art) and which enable it, even years later, to spark memories and recollections, to comfort and reassure.

To give something is to enrich and transform it, to burden it with affection or love which, however, it bears effortlessly — an act of transformation that depends for its completion on the recipient. (To reject a gift is to strip it of that added value, to reduce it to being, once more, only what it appears.) What is added to something when it is chosen as a gift could not be better illustrated than by the following response to a question on what things in the home *mean*:

> Love, love. I can say that love covers it all because the people who have given them to me love me or they wouldn't give me such things. It means a whole family, that we all enjoy receiving these things. . . . And if somebody makes it and puts so much time in it, to me it's love that's been put into the object . . . that's more special to me than anything . . . if you know how many hours are put into it.[1]

To be surrounded by gifts is to be surrounded by things which have been charged with love, charged to respond to us, to reflect and enhance our identities; yet in thus responding, they require us to accept and cherish, not to disdain or abuse, them. Thus they stimulate a caring response from us; they invite us to perceive them creatively; to *re*create them (like taking a mechanism apart, lovingly cleaning and rebuilding it so that every piece is remembered and attended to and the mechanism as a whole becomes 'as good as new'); to *cultivate* them. My use of the word 'cultivate' in this context derives from a remarkable book, *The meaning of things: domestic symbols and the self* by Mihaly Csikszentmihalyi and Eugene Rochberg-Halton.[2] What is meant by 'cultivation' (and indeed by 'culture') can be illustrated by our cultivation of plants — attending to and caring for

137

them in such a way as to enable them to grow to their full potential. For Csikszentmihalyi and Rochberg-Halton, the cultivation of things — attending to them, cherishing them, using them as they are meant to be used (tools, musical instruments) — offers a redeeming alternative to 'terminal materialism'; whereas the latter smothers us, and exhausts the world's resources with its own inexhaustible greed to possess and to 'consume', our cultivation of the world and its objects — controlled by the natural limits of what any of us really can use or cultivate properly — enables us to extend and to cultivate ourselves, to see ourselves mirrored in the world, to feel at home in it, members of its family. Thus family and home, community and place, are areas of cultivation, of culture — *ecologies* in which the cultivators are cultivated. Taking family and home as a model, then, family art demonstrates the role of art, and of creativity, in this process of cultivation.

Our relationship with the things around us, and their nature as gifts, have been illuminated — from a startling point of view — by Elaine Scarry in a study of torture. Whereas through family art we give to ourselves and to each other a responsive and comforting world, the repertoire of torture includes depriving victims of artefacts, confining them instead in bare and comfortless surroundings. Scarry's analysis of the nature of this deprivation is informed by her awareness of gifts and of family art:

> It is universally the case in everyday life that the most cherished object is one that has been hand-made by a friend: there is no mystery about this, for the object's material attributes themselves record and memorialize the intensely personal, extraordinary because exclusive, interior feelings of the maker for just this person. This is for you.

And (she goes on to say) even

> anonymous, mass-produced objects contain a collective and equally extraordinary message: Whoever you are, and whether or not I personally like or even know you, in at least this small way, be well.[3]

A chair, for example, offers support and repose. Such objects, however modest, even a fresh coat of paint on a cell wall, can lift the spirits:

> Whether they reach someone in extreme conditions of imprison-
> ment or in the benign and ordinary conditions of everyday life,
> [artefacts] contain within them the wish for well-being: 'Don't
> cry; be warm . . .'[4]

The things we create, Scarry argues, recreate us, which indeed is why we make them; through them we recreate ourselves. By making a chair we endow it with some of the comfort of, say, a mother's lap for an infant; it becomes responsive to our need to sit and rest, and thus, almost alive. Artefacts are a 'fulcrum or lever' across which the force of creation moves from us and back to us:

> The act of human creating includes both the creating of the
> object and the object's recreating of the human being, and it is
> only because of the second that the first is undertaken.[5]

We make clothes and blankets to keep us warm, furniture to make us comfortable; they make us warm and comfortable, and they make of us wearers of clothing and users of furniture. The homes we make make us homely; insofar as and in what manner we create the world, it recreates and confirms us as co-Creators.

But only as *co*-Creators. The world is more than any or all of us put into it; it is enriched by *otherness* — other people, other living things, inanimate matter, infinity, mysteries we cannot fathom, there is more to it than the meanings we write on its pages. Insofar as we create it, it shows to us the world we have made with the world we have been given. Insofar as we can make it homelike, it lends itself to being so made.

The 'cultivation' of a particular house is the inspiration for Lucy Boston's 'Green Knowe' series of children's books, re-ferred to in previous chapters. The house of the books is an imaginative recreation of her own home, a moated Norman hall in East Anglia. The house and its contents, and its garden and grounds, are received in the present as gifts from the past; indeed, it sometimes seems to be the house itself that gives to each generation and each visitor:

139

He put out his hand and touched the china. 'How do you come
to have so many things?'
'It's the house', she said . . .[6]

The spirit of the house embraces and is manifested by its
contents; its rooms, furniture, a family portrait, the toys and
books of earlier generations of children, a special place in the
garden – these are the agents through which identities live on;
the first book, *The Children of Green Knowe*,[7] culminates in a
celebration of Christmas that includes an exchange of the most
carefully chosen, original gifts, between past and present as
well as among the living.

Giving is at the heart of family art, which is in essence a gift,
never complete, constantly accumulating, which the family
gives endlessly to itself. The house is such a gift, only rarely
inherited through generations, almost as rarely genuinely
'home-made', but in any case given again and again, through
its purchase, embellishment, redecoration, rearrangement, and
extension, and through such celebrations as Christmas's
decking out and transforming of it. A room can be the most
wonderful gift. The home accommodates and is enriched by
gifts from members of the family to one another. As the family
gives itself treats and holidays, so also, in acquiring camera
and film, it gives itself the means of recording and enjoying
them after the event. Meals and special occasions, celebrations
and ceremonies, are gifts. Giving, in this spirit and context,
transcends any petty 'rules' of fair exchange; it exempts the
recipient from obligation except insofar as it looks for an echo of
pleasure and delight, a response to the gift that is sufficient
indication that it is appreciated and will be cultivated, to complete the act of giving. If a lot of giving appears to abide by
conventions of exchange, this may not be because of what the
rules insist but simply because the people involved want to give
to one another and to preserve and breathe life into rituals of
mutual giving that facilitate this. Moreover, some family giving,
notably by parents to children, takes place through rituals that
allow parents to give covertly in a way that relieves the children

from any obligation whatsoever to give in return; examples include, most notably, the filling of Christmas stockings, with the assistance of Father Christmas, or the appearance of Easter eggs thanks to the Easter Hare.

Family art contributes to the design and realization of dramas and ceremonies of giving, by which presents are, so to speak, 'gift-wrapped' on a memorable occasion, with which they may be ever after associated, and by which both they and the recipient are made 'special'. This is well illustrated by the elaborate stories and procedures that different traditions and families bring to the giving of Christmas presents, including those presents that come from Father Christmas himself. It was certainly my experience that the costlier presents received later on during that day of days, from parents and families, could never match the delight of waking to find a filled stocking on my bed, of feeling, in the dark, the assorted intriguing bulges through the soft wool, and then unwrapping a series of small wonders one by one in the comfort of my parents' bed. Or consider these modes of giving:

> The pinata is a large hanging papier maché ball or animal shape (in Mexico they are made into beautiful forms – donkeys, pigs, birds, etc) filled with sweets and little toys. One child stands beneath the Pinata, surrounded by his friends (at a safe distance!). He is blindfolded and handed a large stick. His friends turn him round and round then tell him to try to hit the Pinata. After several swats the Pinata breaks and a cascade of toys and sweets are released for his delighted friends.[8]

And not dissimilarly:

> In our family the children have an aunt who makes a special gift for them at Christmas. She brings a large cracker which is laid out on the Christmas table in the evening after tea. It is always arranged with great ceremony. When the children and adults pull from both ends there is a bang as the two balloons inside are pricked with a pin and out scatter a number of little presents carefully wrapped up and there are always two for everyone![9]

– Cascades and explosions of giving, in which the giving becomes a gift in itself.

To give something thoughtfully is to provide for its cultivation: as we say of pets, it is given 'to a good home' in the expectation that it will be cherished. This is as true of the purchased as of the homemade gift, in spite of the fact that in the case of the gift one makes oneself, making and giving fuse into a seamless process, and affection is built into the object as one of its ingredients. A problem here is that, if skill is lacking, for instance, affection may become the principal ingredient to an extent that represents a risk and the possibility of disappointment, because much then depends on the recipient responding to the affection with affection, to the role rather than the form of the gift. Giving involves a creative attitude towards the intended recipient, one of identifying sufficiently with that person to have some inkling of how he or she can best be 'cultivated' (not unlike knowing how and with what in particular to 'feed' a plant); when purchase is contemplated, it involves a creative approach to commodities, in which knowing and caring for someone sufficiently to be able to anticipate their response so informs the choosing, wrapping, and presenting of the gift, as to *recreate* it. What was, for instance, just another flute, is transformed to become Alexander's flute − and with this example I am alluding once more to *The Children of Green Knowe*, in which Alexander's flute is still Alexander's flute two hundred years later, and the very special circumstances in which it was given to him are still recalled.

Family art, then, encompasses both the creating and the *re-creating* of commodities (including houses), it readily embraces the choosing of things to be part of the home whether they are to be 'gifts' in the orthodox sense, or a 'gift' given by the family to itself. (It also includes *receiving*, that is, accepting and appreciating what is 'given' in the broadest sense; receiving the things around us *as if* they are gifts.) Through creative giving and receiving we create and cultivate around ourselves a world which has a more than merely materialistic dimension − it embodies and reflects values; it is charged with love. But for much of our repertoire or vocabulary of giving we have come to depend heavily on manufacturing industry and on commerce − many of us would live in spartan conditions if thrown back on

142

our own resources; many people do live in such conditions because they have only their own resources and are reduced to what cannot be taken away from them. There need be no conflict between creativity and commerce; whereas it is not the role of the latter to dictate what our homes should contain, it has the potential to vastly extend the range of choice available to us, to multiply the likelihood of finding a gift which is 'just right' for a particular individual or home. So long as commerce does try to dictate and persuade, and insofar as 'home-making' can bully or trick us into submission, family art equips us to resist, to choose for the best reasons, independently, and, for example, to perceive and reject the current vogue for 'personalized' products (inscribed with their owner's name) as the cheat it is: the process of giving 'personalizes' the given, invisibly perhaps, but profoundly, in a way which renders an inscribed name shallow and irrelevant.

One of the most rewarding Christmas presents I have ever received was a home-made booklet containing excerpts from a 'Diary of Christmas' kept by my brother, whose gift it was. In it, he noted his irritation at feeling 'an obligation to buy cards and presents', and indeed the journal set out to investigate whether the meaning of Christmas could still be alive in spite of its commercialization. Making a present of his journal, and thus of part of himself, was a marvellously positive response to his dilemma, the more so because it recorded the last time that my father was able to read the Christmas story from Luke's gospel at breakfast on Christmas Morning – a reading which had been part of the family's Christmas for years, a giving, by my father, passing on what was for him the greatest gift of all. Each year arguments rage as to whether Christmas has become too, or entirely, commercial. Again, there need be no conflict here; commerce could contribute to the proper celebration of Christmas without robbing it of a shred of meaning. In fact, commerce's attitude to itself and its products – its sole aim to create profits, not worth – limits and undermines giving: the market is flooded with the tawdry and vulgar, with the products of exploitation and sweated labour, with aggressive and ugly toys for children, with artefacts that mock and tarnish the reputation

143

of *homo faber*, and with objects that only 'conspicuous consumption' could call into being. This state of affairs would cease overnight if the manufacturing and retail industries adopted a professional ethic, and if that ethic was breathed through by the spirit of giving, and of Christmas as a festival of giving; I do not, of course, mean to imply that commodities should be given away, but rather, that those responsible for the production and marketing of consumer goods should set themselves some, or higher, standards covering all aspects of their products and activities; that they should consider and redefine their role, as a *service*; that they should ask themselves, for instance, whether their products are fit to be left in a child's stocking by Father Christmas, or presented by the Magi to the Infant Christ. (My brother's 'Diary of Christmas' suggests that costlier presents should be given, not on Christmas Day, but at Epiphany, as in fact is the custom in some cultures.)

What, finally, of ownership and the desire to *possess* that is so entangled with our attitudes to home and that commerce inflames and turns to greed? Giving and receiving are part of a process of *per*ceiving and of 'cultivating' things: nurturing the fulfilment of everything they are and can be, living with them as companions, using them as they should be used and thus – in the case of the flute – literally breathing life into them, rather than possessing them as mere things. In *The Children of Green Knowe*, Alexander's flute becomes Tolly's flute – without ceasing to be (or to have been) Alexander's. 'I think Alexander has given you his flute' says Mrs Oldknow when, as it were, the spirit of Alexander in the flute helps Tolly to play it. For Tolly it is the more precious because it was and will never cease to have been Alexander's: Alexander's stewardship of it added to it – the flute acquired the tunes that Alexander played on it and that Tolly learns to play too. The identities of both donor and recipient are involved with, enhanced, commemorated, cultivated, and reflected by, the gift. Yet (to continue with the same example) the flute is not reduced to a hollow vessel to be filled with associations; it is not just a bright surface reflecting a world outside itself. For both Alexander and Tolly it is FLUTE,

144

a unique flute and the essence of flute, its potential explored and released (and, yes, cultivated) by their playing it.[10]

The light with which family art illumines giving and owning shows a way of 'possessing' things lightly, cherishing them for what they are and for the extra meaning they have been given, not squeezing the life out of them or severing them from their source. That the things that mean most to us are *given*, should not stimulate us to go out and grab; that we only have to see things as if they are gifts (as in a sense they are) to experience their capacity to reassure us of *our* reality, should suggest to us that nothing more is needful to make them ours (in a profounder sense than legal ownership can offer).

To sum up, then. Characteristic of family art is a process of giving that is consciously intended or is likely to cultivate recipient, giver, and gift. For parents to give a room to a child, for instance, is to create a place in which the child can grow; some of the potential of the room as a room will thus be realized; finally, the parents themselves will be reflected in, confirmed by, the room and their child's inhabiting of it. (A room I re-arranged for our youngest son while he was in hospital, and that features a model railway along three sides, constantly surprises me with the recollection that I, no handyman, actually did it. I think he likes it too!) Family art encompasses receiving things around us as given, appreciatively, making the most of them, as the Dutch received the daylight that flooded into their houses; it involves adding to what is given, through what we make or choose to acquire; it comprises a recreating of all of these things into a home, a world that we give to one another and in which people, pets, and objects benefit each other in an ecology of interrelationship. By its example it commends to us that we receive the Earth in a similar spirit, and contribute to making it home for its and all our sakes. But perhaps a note of caution is appropriate. Whereas it is possible to cultivate things, and ourselves, in the home, cultivation and *domestication* are not the same. To be fully human we need, sooner or later, to extend ourselves beyond home; whereas it can be hard for parents to release their children into the larger world, love prevents them from not doing so. To domesticate can be to imprison, to

145

confine, to retard rather than to cultivate, to fail to perceive someone or something for what they really are and can be — like keeping a wild creature as a pet, or destroying a landscape of limestone pavement to supply curiously shaped boulders for domestic rockeries. To conceive of the world as home cannot mean to make of it an endless suburb, for that would neither satisfy our human requirements of it as our home (and garden), nor would it allow the world to be home for all its creatures and constituents, the family to which we belong.

14

But is it Art?

Art is essentially a process of giving; the work of art is a gift. It can, of course, be bought and sold; for professional artists, art is a means of earning a living. But no one chooses to be an artist for the sake of material reward. Rather, artists are *chosen*, by having received the gift of creativity in particularly ample measure. 'The artist is not a special kind of person' (in Coomaraswamy's words) – *except* insofar as he or she is *especially* creative; it is nonetheless true that everyone 'is a special kind of artist'. And of all gifts, the gift of creativity most powerfully insists on being passed on; it will not leave its recipients alone but fills them with its divine restlessness; an artist is not an artist who does not feel an urge to share, to communicate, to enhance the world, and augment our common heritage.[1]

Some of the activities that I have categorized as 'family art' either resemble, or have some clear relationship with, the activities of recognized artists. For instance, we have traced the ancestry of family snapshots back to family portraits on canvas painted by, in some cases, the most distinguished artists of the day; rather more hesitantly, we compared Mrs Roberts' 'haymaking' with certain manifestations of contemporary art. A good deal of family art is self-evidently art in a generous, catch-all sense of the word as a description of such activities as painting and drawing irrespective of whether they produce 'masterpieces'. Family art may be the product of the skilled exercise of a *craft*, but it does not insist on either skill (though it can benefit from it) or 'taste', and so can include work which is amateurish and inept. What can certainly be said is that family art is in one respect truer to the nature of art as gift and as a sharing of the gift of creativity, than art which is conceived as, or too readily allows itself to become, a commodity.

I take art to be the *making* of something that is not exclusively 'personal' and that is more or other than merely utilitarian: an 'outward and visible sign' of . . . well, of what is at least universally or extensively valid, over and above 'usefulness'. I would suggest that the *making* may well involve craft, but also, that craft virtuosity does not necessarily result in art; that art can begin, and may, more rarely, achieve fulfilment, without craft; and that 'the crafts' should not automatically be separated from 'art' and accorded a lowlier status because craft products are useful: explicitly or implicitly, they may also *signify*. I suggest, too, that making can include the 'lifting up', by a bodily act or by an act of attention and perception, of 'found' or given objects, in a way that gives them new or renewed significance. This can involve removing them from one context and placing them in another (Duchamp's 'ready-mades' may spring to mind as an instance of this, although I also have in mind the lover who cuts a rosebud to give to his sweetheart, or the bringing of flowers or of stones from a beach into the house). Finally, the something made may be, not simply what is obviously an artefact, made to last, but an environment, a 'happening', an event, a ritual, a visible form of any kind.

These notes towards a definition of art owe a good deal to the artist and writer David Jones who also spoke of art in terms of 'Things set up, lifted up, or in whatever manner made over to the gods'. Art, in other words, involves receiving (of Creation and of creativity, as if they are gifts), cultivating, and giving which is also a giving back. Family art, which though it can certainly help to provide comfort (and in more than the physical sense), is by definition not merely utilitarian. This is made clear by David Jones who, searching for an apt example of what, to him, art essentially is, alighted upon, not a Rembrandt or the Taj Mahal, but the making and decorating of a birthday cake — family art!

. . . If the cook should say 'This is for Susan's birthday – don't you think it a work of art?' you may not agree with the cook's notion of beauty but you would not be able to deny the 'art'.[2]

Art, he argues, is the making of things that in some way 'signify', and, which, as in this case, may recall the past, look forward into the future, and link particular with universal experience. Thus:

all the conditions determining what is art from what is not, are more than fulfilled. There is making, there is added making, there is explicit sign, there is showing forth, a re-presenting, a recalling and there is gratuitousness and there is full intention to make this making thus. Moreover this particular making signifies a birth. It recalls a past event and looks back at some anniversaries and looks forward to future anniversaries, it is essentially celebrative and festal: it would be gay. For as Poussin said of another art: 'The goal of painting is delight'. And this is universally true of all art no matter how difficult it is to posit the delight. But this making, though joyful and celebrative of a birthday, recalls also, by implication, a day, or many days, of at least some degree of acute pain, perhaps of great anguish, and, perhaps, even of death. So that this making covers, in a rudimentary way, or contains in embryo, all that is shown forth in the greatest imaginable art-works.[3]

Among his other works, David Jones produced a number of inscriptions, many of them as gifts for particular friends, in some cases made to mark occasions such as a first communion. That they are art no one would dispute, yet he himself expressed reservations:

. . . I do regard them as essentially 'amateur' and 'personal'. In a sort of way they are 'private'. It would be fatal for anybody to base anything on them. That is why I'm shy of any publicity with regard to them. It is not modesty nor, I hope, false modesty. I'm not convinced that they are good for chaps at large![4]

Do these statements seem to contradict one another – the claims for the birthday cake on the one hand, and the modesty regarding his own, very accomplished inscriptions on the other? Very well, they contradict each other – yet the contradiction is resolved, I believe, in David Jones's perception of art as a 'song of degrees': because something is not *great* art, it is not therefore to be excluded from the world or the family of art altogether; art can begin 'in a rudimentary way'; it can embrace universal themes 'in embryo'.

Undoubtedly much family art could be said to fall within the German category of *Trivialkunst*. But the point is, not that family art is trivial, but that it may appear trivial *from the outside*. Eske Mathiesen tells how an art historian, Julius Lange, was bewildered by what he regarded as a worthless pencil sketch hanging in a friend's house, which turned out to be a sketch of the friend's birthplace, happened upon by chance and subsequently greatly treasured. Elsewhere Mathiesen writes that:

> Entering a home for the first time is like coming to a foreign land. The pictures are so strange, the things are different. But if you stay in the land long enough, you will see that the feelings which hold the human beings together and are bound up with the pictures, are similar to those you have felt yourself. And then you start to look at the pictures with a new interest; you may even learn something new about yourself and your own tradition.[5]

Family art flourishes in private; it belongs in its home: and yet it can also have public or semi-public aspects and functions. But also, particularities can proclaim generalities: love of *a* home is personal, love of *home* is universal. So it is not always possible to draw a sharp distinction between work that is merely personal and private, work that yearns to speak to a wider audience, and work that embodies and conveys universal values.

Howard Becker has drawn attention to the existence of 'art worlds' that 'define the boundaries of acceptable art'. The world of art pundits is, in its own eyes, and in the eyes of many onlookers, *the* art world; one of its primary functions is to translate selected works of art into commodities, choosing and grading them for the marketplace; it supports and bolsters (and preserves) its choice with all the paraphernalia of art criticism, art galleries, and so forth. Artists themselves are only admitted on sufferance, with the exception of the few who are selected to be 'packaged' as 'stars'. It *excludes*

> many people whose work closely resembles work accepted as art. We can see, too, that art worlds frequently incorporate at a later date works they originally rejected, so that the distinction must lie not in the work but in the ability of an art world to accept it and its maker.[6]

Interestingly, Becker uses quilt-making as an example of an art made outside the professional art world but later accepted by it. 'Quilts were not art because no one treated them like art'. One reason why no one treated them like art was because they were made in the home, which no one recognized as an art world; similarly, one reason why so much of what women have made has not been treated like art has been because it has been made in the home. Much the same point is made by Rozsika Parker and Griselda Pollock, who argue that:

> what distinguishes art from craft in the hierarchy [of the arts] is not so much different methods, practices and objects but also *where these things are made, often in the home, and for whom they are made, often for the family.* [My italics][7]

There is some over-simplification here, in a failure to recognize that 'crafts' (and indeed a great deal of creative work of many kinds), whether by women *or men*, are still regarded as different in kind, and as lower in status, than the so-called 'fine arts'; the reasons for this are complex but important, and involve social, class, and even racial as well as gender issues. But in identifying the fine arts, on the one hand, with a particular 'art world', and what we have been calling family art, on the other hand, with a different sphere not recognized as an 'art world', Parker and Pollock are accurate and illuminating:

> The fine arts are a public, professional activity. What women make, which is usually defined as 'craft', could in fact be defined as 'domestic art'. The conditions of production and audience for this kind of art are different from those of the art made in a studio and art school, for the market and gallery. It is out of these different conditions that the hierarchical division

151

between art and craft has been constructed; it has nothing to do with the inherent qualities of the object nor the gender of the maker.[8]

And thus Parker and Pollock can expose the absurdity of the 'discovery' of quilts as 'art': that is, they only become art when hung in an art gallery; on a bed in the home they remain merely quilts:

> The role of the maker has had to be reduced and the processes of production either sentimentalized or suppressed entirely because their connections with the traditional notions of craft might get in the way of an interpretation of quilts as art.[9]

What a devastating comment on art, if to qualify for endorsement an artefact has to be removed from the real world to which it belongs, and brought instead into an 'art world' that is a kind of holy of holies (apart from its decidedly unholy reduction of all art to commodities)!

Family art and its capacity for cherishing and 'cultivating' the things around us, can help us to keep our eyes open and our seeing as free as possible from prejudice and preconception — from the conditioning of the 'art world'. And the notion of art worlds can help our understanding of family art. Thus, if we ask of family art, 'is it art?', we are in danger of looking at it from the narrow perspective of what I have referred to (in mock deference to its own pretensions) as *the* art world; of removing it, conceptually if not in fact, like quilts, from *its* world to a different world in which aesthetic virtues exist in a vacuum. That can lead to appreciation of sorts; it cannot lead to appreciation enriched by understanding; it prevents appreciation, or fulfilment, of the purposes of family art, or of the relationship between different artefacts and aspects of family art that together make up a home. To appreciate family art properly, we must enter its world, an art world of another kind in which art as gift and vehicle for giving enhances family life and tradition, and in which craft skills (where they exist) and freedom and encouragement to create are passed on, as is life itself, from generation to generation. Here quality is not irrelevant:

152

I'm glad Molly got to show you that quilt, but I won't let her sell it. That's the finest thing we ever had in this house. That's the best one she ever done. We had that one on our bed from the first till I told her to put it away for safekeeping.[10]

On the other hand, quality is not all. As Becker remarks:

When we attend someone's birthday party, we customarily sing 'Happy Birthday' to him. We do not hire professional performers for such an event. It doesn't matter if the singing is out of tune or tempo, as long as the song gets sung.[11]

In family art, what matters above all is that 'the song gets sung'. Home is a 'world', in which art can begin and grow. It is, moreover, a world in which art is integrated with everything else; a world indeed to the fashioning and to the *significance* of which art constantly contributes, not exclusively but as part of the process of living and making. And it is thus that family art offers a model for a 'homelike world' and demonstrates how the arts should function worldwide.

In the later stages of writing this book I found myself becoming preoccupied by the question: what light can family art shed on the idea and the prospect of a more homelike world? Driven by something in my character that compels me to look for answers to life's larger questions in whatever material is to hand, I drafted and redrafted a tortuous final chapter that sought solutions to contemporary homelessness, and endeavoured to find a way of averting the kind of global catastrophe that could render the whole world definitively unhomelike, in the values that are represented by family art. Mercifully that chapter is no more. Yet something can be said.

Family art is nourished by creativity that, to a greater or lesser degree, is in all of us, and that can help us to give shape and meaning to our individual lives. Through creativity we interpret and recreate the world around us; in a sense, we make our own worlds. Family life represents a converging of individual worlds (the world of one's own room, of diaries, of the nurturing of a sense of self), and an inhabiting and enhancing of the common ground between them, in the creation of a shared world that itself opens onto and interacts with the larger worlds and perspectives of community, nation, and humankind. Now, while it would be blind and foolish to pretend that this converging of worlds is ever easy or is invariably harmonious, yet, especially if creativity is allowed to play its part, there need be no conflict. Creativity of itself leads to pluralism, to a *social* pluralism that cannot be reduced to everyone for himself or herself; far from being intrinsically competitive, creativity depends upon mutual support, appreciation and understanding: in its essence – as we have seen – it has to do with *giving*. Creativity would not get anywhere if people constantly cancelled out each other's efforts. It fulfils itself through our every uniqueness.

Self and identity have featured prominently in this study of family art, not, however, as manifestations of isolated spirits at odds with each other, but in a context of conviviality, of mutual support and nourishment, of society, of civilization. We discover and create ourselves in order to give of ourselves; without self, we have nothing to give; without self-confidence, we dare not give anything away let alone 'empty ourselves'. Yet giving, emptying ourselves, we do not cease to be ourselves; on the contrary, we are enriched by the fulfilment of our capacity to give. Parents – through family art – give of themselves in creating a world of home for their children (a world in which the children's own capacity to give and to create is nurtured). A 'warm' family is a family that gives of itself, whose creativity overflows; it is a family which cultivates self-confidence as an ability to feel 'at home' in the world *coupled with* a sensitivity to the plight of others. Following on this train of thought, then, a 'homelike world' can be envisaged as a product of *kenosis*, of self-emptying, of giving; created by giving, it is a world whose inhabitants can feel given to but which offers scope for their giving also.

This book has by and large focused on a relatively particular concept of home, the kind of home – middle class, bourgeois, rooted in European tradition – with which I am myself most familiar. Clearly, those who identify homeliness with a particular way of life which, however, they regard as *their* privilege, do nothing to further a more homelike world. But neither can such a world be achieved by imposing any one concept of home. (The most insidious enemy of the values implicit in family art may well be bourgeois greed, the tendency of the relatively fortunate to want *more of the same*; to keep values for one's own exclusive use, or to pin them too securely to familiar, material, manifestations, is to prevent them from fulfilling themselves *as* values, from attaining universality.[12]) A homelike world must be home to us all; indeed, it must accommodate *wildness*, including every variety of natural habitat, both as home for creatures and living things other than ourselves, and to provide us with a more complete home (in which wild Nature fascinates the scientist as well as inspiring the artist in all of us).

A homelike world is a 'craft cultivated by all its members'. A more homelike world would be, not a world defined on our behalf by politicians or planners or the media, not a world the history of which is the history of power and the powerful, but a world in which everyone articulated their own experience, told their own history, shaped their own environment, and were assured of their place in the global family album. A more homelike world must be one in the continuing Creation of which we are involved; that includes, and is enriched by, all our 'worlds'; of which we are houseproud, and in which we are not ashamed to see ourselves reflected.

The question is, then, not whether all or any family art is Art, but whether we are or can become one family – in which case it would surely become less imperative to separate 'Art' from the arts and crafts of ordinary, creative, everyday life, for indeed, *all* art would be family art.

TIEN HSIA IH CHIA

'Under heaven one household'[13]

155

Notes

Chapter 1 What Is Family Art?

1 Eske Mathiesen, 'Libraries and folk art'. *Art Libraries Journal*, Summer 1982, 6 (2), pp. 5–11.

2 Eske Mathiesen, 'Family art', in *Family art: essays and a bibliography to accompany an exhibition*, ed. Philip Pacey. Preston: Preston Polytechnic, 1982, pp. 5–6.

3 Amy Kotkin, 'The family photo album as a form of folklore', *Exposure*, March 1978, 16 (1), pp. 4–8. See also: *Family folklore*, ed. Holly Cutting-Baker et al., Washington, D.C.: Smithsonian Institution, 1976.

4 Walt Whitman, 'There Was a Child Went Forth', *Leaves of Grass*, 1855.

5 Found in a scrapbook discarded by the previous owners of a house he had moved into by Michael Owen Jones, and included in his essay 'L.A. ad-ons and re-dos: renovation in folk art and architectural design', in *Perspectives on American folk art*, eds Ian M. G. Quimby and Scott T. Swank. New York: W. W. Norton, 1980, pp. 325–63. Jones deduces that the 11-year-old of 1936, grown-up and married, must have been disillusioned by her inability to make the kind of home she had once dreamed of: neither the kind of house she had left, modern and mean and without nooks and crannies, nor the necessity to keep moving, permitted it.

6 Elizabeth Gaskell, *North and South*, 1855.

7 Witold Rybczynski, *Home: a short history of an idea*, New York: Viking, 1986; London: Heinemann, 1988, p. 17.

8 Ibid., pp. 17–18.

9 J. H. S. Bossard and E. S. Boll, 'Family ritual and the family

cycle', *Ritual in family living*. Philadelphia: University of Pennsylvania Press, 1950, pp. 135–53.

10 See, for example, Edward Shorter, *The making of the modern family*. London: Collins, 1976.

11 Phillipe Aries, *Centuries of childhood*. London: Cape, 1962. Originally published as *L'Enfant et la vie familiale sous l'Ancien Régime*, Paris: Librairie Plon, 1960.

12 See especially John Lukacs, 'The bourgeois interior', *American Scholar*, Autumn 1970, 39 (4), pp. 616–30; reprinted in the same author's *The passing of the modern age*. New York: Harper and Row, 1972.

13 For the history of childhood, see, for example, Linda A. Pollock, *Forgotten children: parent–child relations from 1500–1900*. Cambridge: Cambridge University Press, 1983. Pollock points out that, just because a previous age did not share precisely the same concept of childhood as our own, that does not mean that it did not have *any* concept of childhood. The same applies, of course, to other groups and cultures, past and present, and to other concepts, such as, for example, the family.

14 Käte Gläser, *Das Bildnis im Berliner Biedermeier*. Berlin: Rembrandt Verlag, 1932; cited in Mario Praz, *Conversation pieces: a survey of the informal group portrait in Europe and America*. London: Methuen, 1971, p. 27.

Chapter 2 Images of Family and Home: Peeping into the Past

1 Huizinga, quoted by John Lukacs, 'The bourgeois interior', *American Scholar*, Autumn 1970, 39 (4), pp. 616–30; reprinted as Chapter 18 of the same author's *The passing of the modern age*. New York: Harper and Row, 1970.

2 Diane Owen Hughes, 'Representing the family: portraits and purposes in Early Modern Italy', *Journal of Interdisciplinary History*, Summer 1986, XVII (1), pp. 73–81; Witold Rybczynski, *Home: a short history of an idea*, New York: Viking, 1986; London: Heinemann, 1988, pp. 20–2.

3 Philippe Aries, *Centuries of childhood*. London: Cape, 1962, p. 349.

4 Oliver Goldsmith, *The Vicar of Wakefield*. 1766.

5 In the Osterreichische Galerie, Vienna and reproduced in Geraldine Norman, *Biedermeier painting 1815–1848*. London: Thames and Hudson, 1988, pp. 36–7.

6 Alice Van Leer Carrick, *Shades of our ancestors*. Boston: Little, Brown and Co., 1928, p. 51.
7 Caroline Davidson, *The world of Mary Ellen Best*. London: Chatto and Windus, 1985.
8 See, for example, Diana Sperling, *Mrs Hurst dancing and other scenes from Regency life*. London: Gollancz, 1981; Daphne Foskett, *John Harden of Brathay Hall*. Kendal: Abbot Hall Art Gallery, 1974; Susan Lasdun, *Victorians at home*. London: Weidenfeld and Nicolson, 1981 (for sketches by John Harden and the Drummond family).
9 Angus Wilkie, *Biedermeier*. London: Chatto and Windus, 1987.
10 Mario Praz, *An illustrated history of interior decoration*. London: Thames and Hudson, 1982, pp. 232—5.
11 Witold Rybczynski, *Home: a short history of an idea*. New York: Viking, 1986; London: Heinemann, 1988, pp. 20—2.
12 Aries, op. cit., p. 334; quoted by Lukács, op. cit., pp. 623—4.
13 Rybczynski, op. cit., p. 58.
14 William Temple, *Observations upon the United Provinces of the Netherlands*; quoted by Rybczynski, ibid., p. 72.
15 Rybczynski, ibid., p. 72.
16 Charles Dickens, *American notes*, London: Chapman and Hall, 1901, p. 105; quoted by James Ayres. *The art of the people in America and Britain 1750—1950*. Manchester: Cornerhouse, 1985, p. 7.
17 Dickens, ibid., p. 108.
18 Edward Shorter, *The making of the modern family*. London: Collins, 1976, especially pp. 124—7.
19 Philip Pacey, 'The poor man's Claude Lorraines: unravelling the story of the dissemination of an image'. *Visual Resources*, 1988, 5 (1), pp. 17—31, color plates I and II.
20 A. J. Lewery, *Narrow boat painting*. Newton Abbot: David and Charles, 1974, especially pp. 88—92.
21 Patricia Patterson, 'Aran kitchens, Aran sweaters'. *Heresies*, Winter 1978, no. 4, pp. 89—92.
22 Ibid., pp. 89—92.

Chapter 3 'Homemaking'

1 Christina Hardyment, *Dream babies*. London: Cape, 1983, p. xii.
2 Clifford Edward Clark, Jr., *The American family home 1800—1960*. Chapel Hill and London: University of North Carolina Press,

1986. I am indebted to this book for much of my information on American homes and 'homemaking'.

3 *The illustrated family Christian almanac for the United States*. New York: American Tract Society, 1850, p. 18.
4 Sereno E. Todd, *Todd's country homes and how to save money*. New York: J. D. Denison, 1870, p. 33.
5 Louis H. Gibson, 'Architecture and the people', *New England Magazine*, 18 March 1898, pp. 21–5.
6 *Artistic homes or how to furnish with taste*. London: Ward Lock, 1881, p. 9.
7 Ibid., p. 117.
8 Ibid., p. 118.
9 Ibid., p. 74.
10 Ibid., p. 75.
11 Eliza Haweis, *The art of decoration*. London: Chatto and Windus, 1881, p. 21.
12 Ibid., p. 23.
13 Ibid., p. 407.
14 Ibid., p. 21.
15 John Durand, 'French domestic life and its lesson'. *Atlantic Monthly*, August 1881, no. 48, pp. 164–78.
16 Neil McKendrick, John Brewer, and J. H. Plumb, *The birth of a consumer society: the commercialization of eighteenth-century England*. London: Europa, 1982.
17 Joseph Tucker, quoted in McKendrick, op. cit., pp. 25–6.
18 William Cobbett, *Rural rides*, 25 October 1825, p. 226.
19 Robert Roberts, *The classic slum*. Manchester: Manchester University Press, 1971, p. 18.
20 Clark, op. cit., p. 127.
21 Theodore Veblen, *The theory of the leisure class*. New York and London: Macmillan, 1899, pp. 68–101.
22 Frank Baum, *The Wizard of Oz*. 1900.
23 Peter Lloyd Jones, 'A taste of class', *Architectural Review*, February 1979, CLXV (984), pp. 72–9.
   See also: Helena Barrett and John Phillips, *Suburban style: the British home 1840–1960*, London: Macdonald Orbis, 1987; Paul Oliver, Ian Davis and Ian Bentley, *Dunroamin: the suburban semi and its enemies*. London: Barrie and Jenkins, 1981; Nicholas Taylor, *The village in the city*. London: Temple Smith, 1973.
24 Mark Twain, *Life on the Mississippi*. 1883.
25 Gervase Wheeler, *Rural homes: or, sketches of houses suited to*

American country life, with original plans, designs, &c. New York: Charles Scribner, 1851, p. 277.

26 Jane Austen, *Mansfield Park*. 1814.

27 Christopher Alexander, Sara Ishikawa and Murray Silverstein, with Max Jacobson, Ingrid Fiksdahl-King and Shlomo Angel, *A pattern language: towns, buildings, construction*. New York: Oxford University Press, 1977, pp. 1164—6.

Chapter 4   A 'Labour of Love'

1 Jonathan F. Stearns, *Female influence, and the true Christian mode of its exercise*. Newburyport, Mass., 1837. Quoted in C. Kurt Dewhurst, Betty MacDowell and Marsha MacDowell, *Artists in aprons: folk art by American women*. New York: Dutton, 1979, pp. 38—9.

2 Roszika Parker, *The subversive stitch*. London: The Women's Press, 1984, p. 69.

3 Ibid., p. 24.

4 E. Warren and Mrs Pullan, *Treasures of needlework*. London: Ward Lock, 1855; quoted by Parker, op. cit., pp. 154—5.

5 Pen Dalton, 'Housewives, leisure crafts and ideology: de-skilling in consumer crafts', in *Women and craft*. London: Virago, 1987, pp. 31—6.

6 Charles Kingsley, *Glaucus: or the wonders of the shore*. Cambridge, 1855, pp. 4—5; quoted by Parker, op. cit., p. 65.

7 Lucy R. Lippard, 'Making something from nothing: towards a definition of women's "hobby art"'. *Heresies*, 1978, IV, pp. 62—5.

8 See for instance: Rachel Maines, 'Fancywork: the archeology of lives', *Feminist Art Journal*, Winter 1974—5, pp. 1 & 3; Roszika Parker and Griselda Pollock, 'Crafty women and the hierarchy of the arts', *Old mistresses: women, art and ideology*. London: Routledge and Kegan Paul, 1981, chapter 2; *Miriam Schapiro: a retrospective 1953—1980*. Wooster, Ohio: College of Wooster Art Museum, 1980.

9 Jane Grey Swisshelm, *Half a century*. Chicago: Jansen, McClury & Co., 1880, pp. 47—60; quoted in Dewhurst, op. cit., pp. 42—3.

10 'Art-work for women III', *Art Journal*, 1872, p. 130. See also: Isabelle Anscombe, *A woman's touch: women in design from 1860 to*

the present day, London: Virago, 1984; Anthea Callen, *Angel in the studio: women in the Arts and Crafts Movement 1870–1914*, London: Astragal Books, 1979.

11 Margurite Ickis, *The standard book of quilt making and collecting*. New York: Dover, 1960, p. 270.

12 Melissa Meyer and Miriam Schapiro, 'Waste not want not', *Heresies*, 1978, IV, pp. 66–9.

13 Lippard, op. cit.

14 Robert Roberts, *A ragged schooling: growing up in the classic slum*, Manchester: Manchester University Press, 1976, p. 30.

15 Almira Phelps, 'Observations on an infant', appended to Albertine Necker de Saussure, *Progressive Education*. Boston, 1835. Quoted in Christina Hardyment, *Dream babies*, London: Cape, 1983, p. 75.

16 Agnes and Kate Walker, 'Starting with rag rugs: the aesthetics of survival', in *Women and craft*, London: Virago, 1987, p. 27.

17 Lippard, op. cit., p. 65.

18 Gillian Clarke, *Letter from a far country*, Manchester: Carcanet New Press, 1982.

19 Caroline M. Hill, 'The economic value of the home', *Journal of Political Economy*, June 1904, no. 12, pp. 408–19.

Chapter 5   At Home with the Larssons

1 Ulf Hård af Segerstad, 'The ideal Swedish home', in *Carl Larsson*. New York: Holt, Rinehart and Winston (for the Brooklyn Museum), 1982, p. 46.

2 Fiona MacCarthy, ' "Nice work by nice people": family art in the Arts and Crafts Movement', in *Family art*, ed. Philip Pacey. Preston: Preston Polytechnic, 1982, pp. 10–13.

3 Carl Larsson, *Ett hem*. Stockholm: Albert Bonniers Forlag, 1899; *Larssons*, Stockholm: Albert Bonniers Forlag, 1902; *Spadarvet*. Stockholm: Albert Bonniers Forlag, 1906; *At solsidan*. Stockholm: Albert Bonniers Forlag, 1910.

English language editions include: Carl Larsson, *Our home*, London: Methuen, 1976; *Our family*, London: Methuen, 1980.

4 Madeleine von Heland, 'Karin and Carl Larsson', in *Carl Larsson*, op. cit., p. 53.

Chapter 6   Mirrors and Memories

1 For this information I am indebted to the Manchester Studies Unit, Manchester Polytechnic.
2 Brian Coe, *The snapshot photograph: the rise of popular photography*. London: Ash and Grant, 1977. Alan Self, 'The family album: means and results', in *Leisure in the twentieth century*. London: Design Council, 1977, pp. 32–7.
3 Eske Mathiesen, 'Family art', in *Family art: essays and a bibliography to accompany an exhibition*, ed. Philip Pacey, Preston: Preston Polytechnic, 1982, pp. 5–6.
4 Ibid., pp. 5–6.
5 Phoebe Lloyd, 'Posthumous mourning portraiture', in *A time to mourn: expressions of grief in nineteenth century America*, ed. Martha V. Pike and Janice Gray Armstrong. Stony Brook, New York: The Museums at Stony Brook, 1980, pp. 71–89.
6 Lyman Beecher, *The autobiography of Lyman Beecher*, ed. Barbara M. Cross. Cambridge, Mass., 1961, p. 127.
7 Richard Rudisill, *Mirror image: the influence of the daguerreotype on American society*. Albuquerque: University of New Mexico Press, 1971. This book is the source of my information on daguerreotypes in America.
8 *Photographic and Fine Art Journal*, January 1855, VIII (1).
9 Ibid., p. 88.
10 Advertisement in *New York Sun* and *New York Tribune*, quoted by Michael Gross, 'The "Wet" and the "Dry"', *Photo Era*, January 1919, XLII, p. 13.
11 *Humphrey's Journal*, 15 January 1854, V (19), p. 297.
12 Heather Spears, *Drawings from the newborn: poems and drawings of infants in crisis*. Port Angeles, Brentwood Bay: Ben-Simon Publications, 1986.
13 *Daguerreian Journal*, 15 January 1851, I (5), p. 149.
14 *American Journal of Photography (New Series)*, 1 June 1858, I(1), p. 9.
15 Atta Gould Woolson, *Woman in American society*. Boston: Roberts Brothers, 1873.
16 *Godey's Lady's Book*, 1860, LX, p. 187.
17 Patricia Cooper, (ed.), *The quilters: women and domestic art: an oral history*. New York: Anchor Press/Doubleday, 1978, p. 17.
18 Ibid., p. 75.
19 Ibid., p. 100.

20 *Always in season: folk art and traditional culture in Vermont*, ed. Jane C. Beck, Vermont Council on the Arts, 1982, pp. 26—7.
21 Published in Gertrude Whiting, *Old-time tools and toys of needle-work*, 1928.
22 Joel and Kate Kopp, *American hooked and sewn rugs: folk art underfoot*. New York: Dutton, 1975, pp. 72—3.

Chapter 7 Making the Most of the Best: The Family Album

1 Mark Twain, *Life on the Mississippi*, 1883.
2 *Family Albums*. Manchester: Manchester Polytechnic, Manchester Studies Unit, 1982, p. 6.
3 Richard Chalfen, 'Cinema naiveté: a study of home moviemaking as visual communication', *Studies in the Anthropology of Visual Communication*, 1975, 2, pp. 87—103.
4 Don Sutherland, 'A good home movie is not necessarily "well made"', *Popular Photography*, October 1971; quoted by Chalfen, ibid.
5 Val Williams, *Women photographers*. London: Virago, 1986, p. 74. Interestingly, Val Williams goes on to show how the imagery of domestic photography, 'transposed by a skilled and technically informed method', was used by photographer Lisa Sheridan in the 1930s to portray the British Royal Family in a way that was reassuring for the British people; how it is used in women's magazines to help editors and authors to project themselves as homely, family-oriented people with whom readers can readily identify; and how it has been used to illustrate babycare manuals with images that 'concentrate on the artless idyll of family life' and that depict babycare as 'light-filled, clean and endlessly rewarding'.
6 Roland Barthes, 'The great family of man', in *Mythologies*. London: Cape, 1972, pp. 100—2.
7 See Amy Kotkin, 'The family album as a form of folklore', *Exposure*, March 1978, 16 (1), pp. 4—8. Kotkin, although confirming that family photographs tend to focus on happy times, is aware that photography is just one of several modes of communicating and remembering within a family, each one of which 'characteristically transmits a slightly different image or part of a family's experience'. Photographs 'display the outwardly happy moments and celebrations' and in doing so affirm

ideals and values. Examining one family album in particular, Kotkin notices how although the photographs were 'almost invariably happy, many of the stories they rekindled were not'; for example, 'A proud photo of Nancy's father in his World War II army uniform was counterpointed with a tragic tale of how he had shot a little boy in Germany, mistaking him for an enemy soldier.'

8 Robert U. Akeret, *Photoanalysis: how to interpret the hidden psychological meaning of personal and public photographs*. New York: Peter H. Wyden Inc., 1973.

9 Ibid.

10 Williams, op. cit., p. 88.

11 Jo Spence, *Putting myself in the picture*. London: Camden Press, 1986.

12 Ibid.

13 Ibid.

14 Mark and Dan Jury, *Gramp*. New York: Grossman Publishers, 1976.

15 Ibid., p. 151.

16 Ibid., p. 151.

17 Ibid., p. 135.

18 Ibid., p. 96.

19 Ibid., pp. vii—viii.

20 Ibid., p. 113.

21 Ibid., p. 144.

22 Ibid., pp. 151—2.

Chapter 8   Marking Time: Ritual and Ceremony

1 James H. S. Bossard and Eleanor S. Boll, *Ritual in family living: a contemporary study*. Philadelphia: University of Pennsylvania Press, 1950.

2 Jeremy Seabrook, *Working-class childhood: an oral history*. London: Gollancz, 1982, pp. 202—8.

3 Gillian Clarke, *Letter from a far country*. Manchester: Carcanet New Press, 1982.

4 Sheila Fell, in *Breakthrough: autobiographical accounts of the education of some socially disadvantaged children*, ed. Ronald Goldman. London: Routledge and Kegan Paul, 1968, pp. 62—3.

5 Lucy Boston, *A stranger at Green Knowe*. London: Faber, 1961, p. 146.

6 Iona and Peter Opie, *The lore and language of schoolchildren*. Oxford: Oxford University Press, pp. 241—3.

7 Patricia Cooper et al. (eds), *The quilters: women and domestic art: an oral history*, New York: Anchor Press/Doubleday, 1978, p. 49.

8 Geoffrey Gorer, *Death, grief and mourning in contemporary Britain*, London: The Cresset Press, 1965, p. 132.

9 Nils-Arvid Bringeus, 'Then and now'. *Form*, 1982, no. 6—7, pp. 6—9 (Swedish journal with English summaries).

10 Robert Roberts, *A ragged schooling: growing up in the classic slum*. Manchester: Manchester University Press, 1976, pp. 24—5.

11 John Lukacs, 'The bourgeois interior'. *American Scholar*, 1970, 39 (4), pp. 616—30; reprinted in the same author's *The passing of the modern age*, New York: Harper and Row, 1972.

12 Bossard and Boll, op. cit., pp. 18—19.

Chapter 9 A Child's World

1 Iona and Peter Opie, *The lore and language of schoolchildren*. Oxford: Oxford University Press, 1959, p. 232.

2 Gaston Bachelard, *The poetics of space*. Boston: Beacon Press, 1969, pp. 14—15.

3 Peter Townsend, *The family life of old people: an inquiry in East London*. London: Routledge and Kegan Paul, 1957, p. 27.

4 John Burnett (ed.), *Destiny obscure: autobiographies of childhood, education and family from the 1820s to the 1920s*. London: Allen Lane, 1982.

5 William Wordsworth, 'Composed by the sea-shore'.

6 O. Lerman, 'Autobiographical journey: can art transform personal and cultural loss', *Arts Magazine*, May 1985, no. 59, pp. 103—7.

7 Astrid Lindgren, *The six Bullerby children*. London: Methuen, 1963.

8 Gertrude Jekyll, *Children and gardens*. London: *Country Life*, Antique Collectors' Club, 1982. (Originally published in 1908.)

9 Robert Roberts, *A ragged schooling: growing up in the classic slum*, Manchester: Manchester University Press, 1976.

10 E. Nesbit, *Wings and the child*. London: Hodder and Stoughton, 1913.

11 *Highroads in geography*, vol. 1. London: Thomas Nelson, 1910.
12 Roberts, op. cit.
13 To give just one example: *The little grey men* by 'B.B.' (Denys Watkins-Pitchford).
14 Among countless examples, Ray Rope's series commencing with *The model railway men* is notable for choosing a model railway — many children's books are centred on dolls' houses — and for the way in which the model railway men (and women) fiercely insist on running the line professionally.
15 Robert Louis Stevenson, 'My Kingdom'. Quoted in Felicity Bryan, *A garden for children*, London: Michael Joseph, 1986, p. 106.
16 Gerald Durrell, *My family and other animals*. London: Hart-Davis, 1956. Quoted in Bryan, op. cit., p. 127.

Chapter 10   Gardens

1 David Crouch and Colin Ward, *The allotment: its landscape and culture*, London: Faber, 1988.
    Crouch and Ward argue that British allotments have been more frequently 'family affairs' — the scene of family picnics as well as of child labour — than their popular image as a husband's retreat suggests. But in Britain, the European and Scandinavian 'leisure garden', conceived and made for the whole family, is the exception rather than the rule. For Danish practice, see Jørgen Haagen, *Kolonihaven*, Copenhagen, 1976; Eske Mathiesen, *Den danske have*, Copenhagen, 1982; and *Kolonihavebogen*. Copenhagen: Politikens Forlag, 1988.
2 Fred E. H. Schroeder, 'The democratic yard and garden', *Outlaw aesthetics: arts and the public mind*. Bowling Green, Ohio: Bowling Green University Popular Press, 1977, pp. 94–122.
3 Ibid.
4 Ibid.
5 John Sedding, *Gardencraft Old & New*. 1891.
6 Peter Lloyd-Jones, 'A taste of class', *Architectural Review*, February 1979, CLXV (984), pp. 72–9. See also Helena Barrett and John Phillips, 'Gardens in suburbia', *The suburban style: the British home, 1840–1960*. London: Macdonald Orbis, 1987, pp. 169–88.

7 Paul Edwards, *English garden ornaments*. London: G. Bell, 1965, p. 117.
8 Bernard Lassus, *Jardins imaginaires*. Paris: Les Presses de la Connaissance, 1977.
9 Jane Brown, *Vita's other world: a gardening biography of Vita Sackville-West*. London: Viking, 1985, p. 196.
10 Gertrude Jekyll, *Children and gardens*. London: Country Life, 1908, p. 145.
11 Ibid., p. 156.
12 Schroeder, op. cit.
13 Ibid.
14 Jekyll, op. cit., pp. 164—87.

Chapter 11 Hospitality and Community

1 Edward Shorter, The making of the modern family. London: Collins, 1976, p. 17.
2 Robert Roberts, *The classic slum*, Manchester: Manchester University Press, 1971, p. 35.
3 Mihaly Csikszentmihalyi and Eugene Rochberg-Halton, *The meaning of things: domestic symbols and the self*. Cambridge: Cambridge University Press, 1981, p. 158.
4 Ibid., p. 170.
5 Ibid., pp. 170—1.
6 Ibid., p. 139.
7 Paul Zumthor, *Daily life in Rembrandt's Holland*. London: Weidenfeld and Nicolson, 1962, pp. 74—5.
8 Simon Schama, *The embarrassment of riches: an interpretation of Dutch culture in the Golden Age*. London: Collins, 1987, p. 393.
9 Ibid., p. 570.
10 John Burnett (ed.), *Destiny obscure: autobiographies of childhood, education and family from the 1820s to the 1920s*. London: Allen Lane, 1982, p. 218.
11 Ibid., pp. 218—19.
12 Renée Hirschon, 'Essential objects and the sacred: interior and exterior space in an urban Greek locality', in *Women and space: ground rules and social maps*, ed. Shirley Ardener. London: Croom Helm, 1981, pp. 72—88.
13 Zumthor, op. cit., p. 96.
14 Schama, op. cit., p. 521.

15 Peter Spier, *Of dikes and windmills*. New York: Doubleday, 1969, pp. 70−2.
16 This picture is in the Hochschule für bildende Künste, Hamburg; it is reproduced in Carla Gottlieb, *The window in art*. Abaris Books, 1981, pp. 291−3.
17 Judith Friedman Hansen, 'The proxemics of Danish daily life', *Studies in the Anthropology of Visual Communication*, 1976, 3 (1), pp. 52−62.
18 Ibid.
19 Ibid.
20 Ibid.
21 Tove Ditlevsen, 'Sjaeldent hyggeligt', in *Om hygge*. Copenhagen: Politikens Forlag, 1965, pp. 9−17. Quoted by Hansen, op. cit.
22 Philip Pacey, 'The poor man's Claude Lorraines: unravelling the story of the dissemination of an image', *Visual Resources*, 1988, V (1), pp. 17−31, colour plates I and II.

Chapter 12   Letting in Infinity

1 See, for example, Paul Oliver, 'Values, symbols and meanings', *Dwellings: the house across the world*. London: Phaidon, 1987, pp. 153−70.
2 Renée Hirschon, 'Essential objects and the sacred: interior and exterior space in an urban Greek locality', in *Women and space: ground rules and social maps*, ed. Shirley Ardener. London: Croom Helm, 1981, pp. 72−88.
3 Ibid.
4 Isaiah 32: 15−20.
5 Martin Buber, *The way of man according to the teaching of Hasidism*. London: Vincent Stuart, 1963, p. 36.
6 Arlene Rossen Cardozo, *Jewish family celebrations: the Sabbath, festivals, and ceremonies*. New York: St Martin's Press, 1982, p. 13.
7 Ibid., p. xii.
8 Ibid., p. 65.
9 Ibid., p. 63.
10 Ibid., p. 69.
11 Ibid., p. 87.
12 Ibid., pp. 90−1.
13 Ibid., p. 226.

14 Ibid., pp. 110−20.
15 Ibid., pp. 162−3.
16 Ibid., p. 130.
17 Lucy Boston, *An enemy at Green Knowe*. London: Faber, 1964, pp. 14−15.
18 Buber, op. cit., p. 41.
19 Mihaly Csikszentmihalyi and Eugene Rochberg-Halton, *The meaning of things: domestic symbols and the self*. Cambridge: Cambridge University Press, p. 192.

Chapter 13   Giving and Perceiving

1 Mihaly Csikszentmihalyi and Eugene Rochberg-Halton, *The meaning of things: domestic symbols and the self*. Cambridge: Cambridge University Press, 1981, p. 143.
2 Ibid.
3 Elaine Scarry, *The body in pain: the making and unmaking of the world*. New York: Oxford University Press, 1985, p. 292.
4 Ibid., p. 292.
5 Ibid., p. 310.
6 Lucy Boston, *A Stranger at Green Knowe*. London: Faber, 1961, p. 68.
7 Lucy Boston, *The Children of Green Knowe*. London: Faber, 1954.
8 Diana Carey and Judy Large, *Festivals, family and food*. Stroud: Hawthorn Press, 1982, p. 162. (Instructions for making *pinata* are given.)
9 Ibid., p. 147.
10 The case of Alexander's flute illustrates an aspect of the proper cultivation of gifts, namely, the responsibility to pass them on, to let them continue to be given and to serve. See Lewis Hyde's remarkable book *The gift: imagination and the erotic life of property*. New York: Random House, 1983.

Chapter 14   But Is It Art?

1 Lewis Hyde, *The gift: imagination and the erotic life of property*. New York: Random House, 1983; Philip Pacey, 'Art as service', *Journal of Arts Policy and Management*, December 1985, 2 (2), pp. 4−7. Reprinted as *Art as service*. Preston: Lancashire Polytechnic, 1988.

2 David Jones, *Epoch and artist*. London: Faber, 1959, pp. 163–4.
3 Ibid., pp. 163–4.
4 David Jones, Letter to Nicolete Gray, 4 April 1961. Quoted in Nicolete Gray, *The painted inscriptions of David Jones*. London: Gordon Fraser, 1981, p. 103.
5 Eske Mathiesen, 'Libraries and folk art', *Art Libraries Journal*, Summer 1982, 6 (2), pp. 5–11.
6 Howard Becker, *Art worlds*. Berkeley and Los Angeles: University of California Press, 1982, p. 227.
7 Roszika Parker and Griselda Pollock, *Old mistresses: women, art and ideology*. London: Routledge and Kegan Paul, 1981, p. 70.
8 Ibid., p. 70.
9 Ibid., p. 75.
10 Quoted by Becker, op. cit., p. 251.
11 Becker, op. cit., p. 246.
12 See John Lukacs, 'The bourgeois interior', *American Scholar*, Autumn 1970, 39 (4), pp. 616–30; reprinted in the same author's *The passing of the modern age*. New York: Harper and Row, 1972.
13 My father recalled these Chinese characters as written on the wall of the church in Kunming where he and my mother were married. Literally 'Under heaven one household', the first two characters can be taken to mean 'The whole world'; my father sometimes translated the whole phrase as 'All under heaven one family' and linked it to Ephesians 4, 4–6.

Bibliography

This book is to the best of my knowledge the first book to be published on family art. As such, it has drawn on a wide range of publications, many of which are acknowledged in the lists of references for each chapter, and I have no doubt that there is much more evidence of family art to be discovered in, for example, autobiographies, or books on folk art. Whereas the primary purpose of my book is to stimulate readers to reflect on their own experience and to release creativity into their lives, this bibliography offers suggestions for any who might wish to pursue further reading on family art or related topics.

Family art: precursors of this book

A number of publications led directly to the present volume. I first came upon the term 'family art' in an article by Eske Mathiesen that I was responsible for publishing in English translation: Mathiesen, Eske, 'Libraries and folk art', *Art Libraries Journal*, Summer 1982, 6 (2), pp. 5–11. This article had originally appeared in Danish, in *Bibliotek*, 1973, 70 (2), pp. 31–4. Similar ground was covered by the same author in 'Folks egne billeder', *DFSNYT 73/4*. Copenhagen: Folke-mindesamling, 1973.

Immediately after reading Eske Mathiesen's article, I made it my business to organize an exhibition of family art, and Eske Mathiesen readily agreed to contribute to an 'exhibition catalogue': Pacey, Philip (ed.), *Family art: essays and a bibliography to accompany an exhibition*. Preston: Preston Polytechnic Library, 1982. (Contents: 'Family art: an introduction', by Philip Pacey; 'Family Art' by Eske Mathiesen; 'The Art of the Home' by James Ayres; ' "Nice work by nice people":

Family Art in the Arts and Crafts Movement' by Fiona MacCarthy; and 'Family Art in Islington' by Shirley Hooper.) The exhibition itself was shown at several locations, including the Bethnal Green Museum of Childhood and the British Film Institute in London, and the Harris Museum and Art Gallery, Preston.

Subsequently I developed my own approach to family art in the following article: Pacey, Philip, 'Family art: domestic and eternal bliss', *Journal of Popular Culture*, 1984, 18 (1), pp. 43–52.

Family culture

The following texts shed significant light on family art.

The Smithsonian Institution's Family Folklore Program has explored the concept of 'family culture' (of which family art is a part): Cutting-Baker, Holly (ed.), *Family folklore, collected by The Family Folklore Program of the Festival of American Folk Life*. Washington, D.C.: Smithsonian Institution, 1976. Although the emphasis is on family *stories*, family traditions and family photography are also referred to and a brief section on 'Other ways families preserve their past' includes needlework and memorabilia and illustrates a magnificent quilt that commemorates one family's history. An expanded version of this volume was published a few years later: Zeitlin, Steven J. and Kotkin, Amy J. (eds), *A celebration of American family folklore: tales and traditions from the Smithsonian Collection*. New York: Pantheon; Toronto: Random House, 1982.

Ritual, an important aspect of both family art and family culture, is the subject of a sympathetic and readable study: Bossard, James H. S. and Boll, Eleanor, S., *Ritual in family living: a contemporary study*. Philadelphia: University of Pennsylvania Press, 1950.

Ritual in Jewish family life is admirably described in: Cardozo, Arlene Rossen, *Jewish family celebrations: the Sabbath, festivals, and ceremonies*. New York: St Martin's Press, 1982.

Funeral rituals and visual expressions of grief are documented by: Pike, Martha V. and Armstrong, Janice Gray (eds), *A time to mourn: expressions of grief in nineteenth century America*. Stony Brook, New York: The Museums at Stony Brook, 1980.

The following article, in characterizing rituals of hospitality and other aspects of family life, provides a valuable tool for analysing the nature of family art: Hansen, Judith Freidman, 'The proxemics of

172

Danish daily life', *Studies in the Anthropology of Visual Communication*, 1976, 3 (1), pp. 56–62.

A fascinating work which sheds a great deal of light on family art is: Csikszentmihalyi, Mihaly and Rochberg-Halton, Eugene, *The meaning of things: domestic symbols and the self.* Cambridge: Cambridge University Press, 1981.

The following study, although perceptive, may not be easily accessible to readers unused to sociological texts: Reiss, David, *The family's construction of reality.* Cambridge, Massachusetts: Harvard University Press, 1981.

Family art is — almost — comprehensively illustrated by the *Larsson family home.* English language editions of Carl Larsson's albums of watercolours include *Our home* (London: Methuen, 1976) and *Our family* (London: Methuen, 1980). The Brooklyn Museum's exhibition catalogue *Carl Larsson* (New York: Holt, Rinehart and Wiston, 1982) is also a valuable source of information. An excellent illustrated guide to the Larsson home at Sundborn is *Der Carl Larsson-Hof* by Ulf Hård af Segerstad (Stockholm: Granath & Hård af Segerstad Förlagsproduktion, 1975).

House and home

Next, material on the *house and home*. Leading the field in its provision of crucial background reading is Witold Rybczynski's account of the evolution of domestic comfort: Rybczynski, Witold, *Home: a short history of an idea.* New York: Viking, 1986; London: Heinemann, 1988.

Other texts follow in alphabetical order:

Alexander, Christopher et al., *A pattern language: towns, buildings, construction.* New York: Oxford University Press, 1977. (A marvellous volume, well worth dipping into for the sections relevant to family and home, and indeed for many other illuminations and inspirations.)

Ayres, James, *The Shell book of the home in Britain: decoration, design and construction of vernacular interiors 1500–1850.* London: Faber, 1981.

Barrett, Helena and Phillips, John, *Suburban style: the British home 1840–1960.* London: Macdonald Orbis, 1987.

Chapman, Dennis, *The home and social status.* London: Routledge and Kegan Paul, 1955.

Clark, Clifford Edward, *The American family home 1800–1960.* Chapel Hill and London: University of North Carolina Press, 1986.

Hayden, Dolores, *Redesigning the American dream*. New York: W. W. Norton, 1984.

Jones, Michael Owen, 'L.A. add-ons and re-dos: renovation in folk art and architectural design', in *Perspectives on American folk art*, eds Ian M. G. Quimby and Scott T. Swank. New York: W. W. Norton, 1980, pp. 325–363.

Jones, Peter Lloyd, 'A taste of class', *Architectural Review*, February 1979, CLXV (984), pp. 72–9.

Lukacs, John, 'The bourgeois interior', *American Scholar*, Autumn 1970, 39 (4), pp. 616–30; reprinted in the same author's *The passing of the modern age*. New York: Harper and Row, 1972.

Oliver, Paul et al., *Dunroamin: the suburban semi and its enemies*. London: Barrie and Jenkins, 1981.

Praz, Mario, *An illustrated history of interior decoration*. London: Thames and Hudson, 1987.

Taylor, Nicholas, *The village in the city*. London: Temple Smith, 1973.

Thornton, Peter, *Authentic decor: the domestic interior 1620–1920*. London: Weidenfeld and Nicolson, 1984.

Family portraits

Praz, Mario, *Conversation pieces: a survey of the informal group portrait in Europe and America*. London: Methuen, 1971. (An unparalleled source for group – and therefore family – portraits.)
Also useful are:

Aries, Philippe, *Centuries of childhood*. London: Jonathan Cape, 1962.

Ayres, James, *English naive painting 1750–1900*. London: Thames and Hudson, 1980. (For 'folk art' portraits in Britain. American folk portraits are illustrated in innumerable books on American folk art.)

Davidson, Caroline, *The world of Mary Ellen Best*. London: Chatto and Windus, 1985. (Doubly useful because of Mary Ellen Best's watercolours of domestic interiors.)

Norman, Geraldine, *Biedermeier painting 1815–1848*. London: Thames and Hudson, 1988.

Family photography

Akeret, Robert U., *Photoanalysis: how to interpret the hidden psychological meaning of personal and public photographs*. New York: Peter H. Wyden Inc., 1973.

Bibliography

Bellof, Hall, 'The fairytale album', *New Society*, 16 May 1985, pp. 226–7.

Chalfen, Richard, 'Cinema naivete: a study of home moviemaking as visual communication', *Studies in the Anthropology of Visual Communication*, 1975, 2, pp. 87–103.

Coe, Brian, *The history of movie photography*. London: Ash and Grant, 1981.

Coe, Brian, *The snapshot photograph: the rise of popular photography*. London: Ash and Grant, 1977.

Family albums. Manchester: Manchester Polytechnic; Manchester Studies Unit, 1982.

Hirsch, Julia, *Family photographs: content, meaning, and effect*. New York: Oxford University Press, 1981.

Isherwood, Sue, *The family album*. London: Channel 4 Television, 1988.

Kotkin, Amy, 'The family album as a form of folklore', *Exposure*, 1 March 1978, 16, pp. 4–8.

Lesy, Michael, *Timeframes: the meaning of family pictures*. New York: Pantheon Books, 1980.

Ohrn, Karin Becker, 'The photo flow of family life: a family photograph collection', *Folklore Forum*, 1975, no. 13, pp. 27–35.

Rudisill, Richard, *Mirror image: the influence of the daguerrotype on American society*. Albuquerque: University of New Mexico Press, 1971.

Self, Alan, 'The family album: means and results', in *Leisure in the twentieth century*. London Design Council, 1977.

Spence, Jo, *Putting myself in the picture*. London: Camden Press, 1986.

Williams, Val, *Women photographers*. London: Virago, 1986.

Womens' creativity in the home

Anscombe, Isabelle, *A woman's touch: women in design from 1860 to the present day*. London: Virago, 1984.

Callen, Anthea, *Angel ·in the studio: women in the Arts and Crafts Movement 1870–1914*. London: Astragal Books, 1979.

Canadian hooked rugs 1860–1960. Montreal: McCord Museum (c. 1977).

Cooper, Patricia et al., *The quilters: women and domestic art: an oral history*. New York: Anchor Press/Doubleday, 1978.

Dewhurst, C. Kurt et al., *Artists in aprons: folk art by American women*. New York: Dutton, 1979.

175

Bibliography

Ickis, Margurite, *The standard book of quilt making and collecting*. New York: Dover, 1960.

Isaacs, Jennifer, *The gentle arts: two hundred years of Australian women's domestic and decorative arts*. Willoughby, New South Wales: Lansdowne Press, 1987.

Kopp, Joel and Kate, *American hooked and sewn rugs: folk art underfoot*. New York: Dutton, 1975.

Lippard, Lucy R., 'Making something from nothing: towards a definition of women's hobby art', *Heresies*, 1978, 4, pp. 62–5.

Maines, Rachel, 'Fancywork: the archeology of lives', *Feminist Art Journal*, Winter 1974–75, pp. 1 & 3.

Meyer, Melissa and Schapiro, Miriam, 'Waste not want not', *Heresies*, 1978, 4, pp. 66–9.

Parker, Roszika, *The subversive stitch*. London: The Women's Press, 1984.

Parker, Roszika and Pollock, Griselda, *Old mistresses: women, art and ideology*. London: Routledge and Kegan Paul, 1981, Chapter 2, 'Crafty women and the hierarchy of the arts'.

Patterson, Patricia, 'Aran kitchens, Aran sweaters', *Heresies*, 1978, no. 4, pp. 89–92.

Robinson, Charlotte (ed.), *The artist and the quilt*. Bromley: Columbus Books, 1983.

Schapiro, Miriam, *Miriam Schapiro: a retrospective 1953–1980*. Wooster, Ohio: College of Wooster Art Museum, 1980.

Weismann, Judith Reiter and Lavitt, Wendy, *Labors of love*. London: Studio Vista, 1988.

Women and craft. London: Virago, 1987.

Index